# Son of a Son of a Politician

Paul Helmke: Behind City Hall doors

# Son of a Son of a Politician

## Paul Helmke: Behind City Hall doors

*12 years as mayor of Indiana's second largest city, Fort Wayne*

*As told to and authored by Andrew Jarosh*

Writers Club Press
San Jose  New York  Lincoln  Shanghai

**Son of a Son of a Politician**
Paul Helmke: Behind City Hall doors

Writers Club Press
an imprint of iUniverse, Inc.

For information address:
iUniverse, Inc.
5220 S. 16th St., Suite 200
Lincoln, NE 68512
www.iuniverse.com

ISBN: 0-595-21600-5

Printed in the United States of America

# CONTENTS

# LIST OF ILLUSTRATIONS

# Editorial Method

Excerpts from the book were published in The Fort Wayne News-Sentinel

# INTRODUCTION

Paul Helmke, an attorney, was Republican mayor of Fort Wayne, Indiana's second largest city, from 1988 to 1999. Not only is this his story, but it's about a conservative Midwestern community coming to grips with the coming of the 21st century.

# It ALL STARTED WITH A YARD SIGN

*Photo by (Courtesy of Paul Helmke)*

**Three generations of Helmkes**

Three generations of Fort Wayne politicians—Paul Helmke, left; his father, Walther P., second from left; and Paul's grandfather, Walter E., far right—stand with then-Indiana Gov. Otis R. Bowen on May 1, 1975, at the local Sheraton Hotel. Bowen wrote, "My very best wishes to three generations of Helmke attorneys."

The whole 1987 campaign came as a surprise to me.

I had grown up liking politics and government, and came from a family that had liked politics and government. I had always seen myself being involved in politics, first as president of my senior class at North Side High School, then as student body president at Indiana University in the late 1960s.

One of the reasons I came back to Fort Wayne after law school was to help my father, Walter, run for Congress in 1974, with an eye toward getting into politics myself. After my father lost, I helped Dan Quayle run for Congress in 1976. He also asked me to run his local office, but I turned him down. I didn't see any political future in it. Meanwhile, in 1980, I ran for Quayle's seat and lost in the primary to Dan Coats, the same guy who took the job to run the local office I had turned down.

After losing in 1980, I thought to myself, "I'm no good at this running for office business and if I'm going to do politics, it's going to be more behind-the-scenes stuff." After May 1980, I didn't have too many political ambitions although I still enjoyed being involved, like with the 1983 city election when Charles "Bud" Meeks lost to Win Moses Jr. for mayor. I stayed active in community organizations but I didn't have anything in mind.

### Mayoral beginnings

At the start of 1987, I had no plans to run for mayor. I had gone to a number of State of the City addresses over the years, and didn't even bother going to the one in 1987. If I were planning to run, I surely would have attended.

Speculation leading into the 1987 election said Moses could be vulnerable because of his campaign finance violations and legal problems from 1985. But the GOP didn't really have anybody in mind to run and Win still seemed to be keeping his popularity high. I really didn't think about running.

County Commissioner Ed Rousseau, who at the time was onCounty Council, was the name mentioned most. He was thinking about it. I remember going to a meeting in January 1987, where I met with Rousseau and Linda Buskirk, who at that time was working for the county commissioners, to discuss the possibility of Rousseau running for mayor. I came out of the meeting thinking it wasn't clear Rousseau wanted to run and that he was more interested running for commissioner.

I was sort of left thinking Rousseau wasn't going to run and no other candidates were coming forward. So, I started thinking maybe I should get involved. I actually considered running for 5th District City Council against Mark GiaQuinta, but I didn't sense Mark was vulnerable. I had been talking to Alan McMahan, who was GOP city chairman at the time, and I'd see him in the morning when I was out jogging. He had always been a political adviser and he told me to keep open my options. I told him I was thinking about running for City Council. He was the first, I believe, who told me I should consider running for mayor.

It was February and still no one had signaled he wanted to run as a Republican. But I felt reluctant to do it. Moses would be difficult to beat. I wasn't sure it was the right kind of life for me. My one daughter was just turning 10, the other was 5. And from a personal side, I wasn't sure I was ready for it.

But I started getting advice from other people. Ernie Williams, former editor at The News-Sentinel, gave me his advice and it was not to run. Instead, he saw my candidacy as an attempt by Orvas Beers, GOP chairman, to tack on another loss to destroy me politically. My father's advice was to not run but back somebody who could win and become city attorney. My wife, Debbie, didn't want me to run, but I was still fascinated by the idea.

It was finally getting down to almost the last day to file. McMahan wanted a decision from me because he'd need a couple of days to get somebody else. Otherwise, it would have looked bad if the filing deadline had passed and the GOP had nobody on the ballot.

## A call to public service

It happened one morning. Former President Gerald Ford had been in town the day before to speak at one of the local high schools. My clock radio turns on, and there's a story about how Ford had been in town telling students they should get involved in the political process. It was sort of a wake-up call hearing that. The message was something I was always telling my daughters. "You always have to get involved." It's what I told elementary and high school students. Politics is something to get involved in.

And it got me thinking. All my life I had been involved in politics and was fascinated by it. I felt it was important to be part of the process. And here was the opportunity to run, and I really had this twinge of conscience, that if I did not do this, it would be selfishness on my part. By not running I was more concerned about keeping up the income level from the law practice, and just having things nice and comfortable, than I was about doing those things you're supposed to do as a good public citizen.

## The decision is made

I decided then that I'm going to do it. I called McMahan and told him I would run. Then I asked him, what should I do next? We set up a time for me to announce. A lot of the local media didn't know who I was. We set up an announcement at the Performing Arts Center, where I made a few comments about how the city had gone in the wrong direction, and that some of Win's problems had hurt Fort Wayne. I also was concerned about the city's finances, and said we needed to get the city again on the right track.

The announcement got good play. But I didn't have a campaign manager, I didn't have a media strategy, I didn't have anything but the willingness to get out there and give it a try.

### 'What have I gotten myself into?'

So that was sort of the start. And then, it was, "What have I gotten myself into?" My wife said she didn't know I was running until she read it in the paper. I probably told her, but she believed we had decided I wasn't going to run. For a lot of people, it was, 'Who is this person?' The name was known more from my father.

For the Republican Party, I was sort of their chosen candidate. My candidacy had the support of the party elders, including Orvas Beers. They sensed, however, it was going to be tough to beat Win. Somebody like me with some sort of name recognition meant I had potential but as a long shot.

Early on, it was tough. I had a busy law practice with cases in progress and client work to do. So, for the first couple of months, it was more of me being a lawyer instead of a campaigner. And I had nothing set up; I relied on the party for everything. We talked about campaign managers, and I finally chose Dan Heath, who had worked for Coats. Heath had come to my candidacy announcement from Coats' office and apparently felt sorry for me. He looked at me as someone who didn't have the slightest idea how to run a campaign. When he found out I didn't have a campaign manager, he couldn't believe it.

But Heath came aboard and it was really a significant choice of someone with campaign experience.

The party did some polling with Bob Teetor, a market opinion pollster, who later became connected with Quayle and former President George Bush. Beers was a friend of Teetor's from a lake cottage in Michigan, and Teetor did some polling for the party. And it showed me way behind in terms of name recognition. But the significant thing I found out was there was some weakness in Moses' support. The challenge for me was to become better known and to engage Moses to make it a contest.

## Engaging the enemy

That last statement ended up being prophetic. It's exactly how things turned out, although at the time, we didn't know how we would do things. The campaign started out slowly because of my work. The first public poll came out around the primary election in May; it showed me behind 2-1. It wasn't very encouraging. In fact I was at a Kentucky Derby party thrown by friends and got a call from a reporter, and I remember asking myself, "How do you spin this?" There isn't much you could do except say there was no place else to go but up.

We started to raise some money, and brought in John Commorato, from Commorato Video, to do media for us. He was somebody interested in trying new ideas. One of the things we did early were video billboards. They were 10- or 15-second commercials, my face and name, and something catchy, like trustworthy or integrity. It would play on Moses' weakness, but also got out the name and face and the "think-about-it line" to voters.

It started to help, along with neighborhood walks. I could really see the difference when the TV ads came out. But things were still going slow. A lot of the local GOP was anti-Moses but they weren't buying into me yet.

## It started with a sign

Then, around July 4, I had done a neighborhood walk and went to my father's lake cottage for the weekend. And then, I read yard signs we had put out violated city ordinance. In June, Heath had bought some yard signs. I had believed the signs were a waste of money. I believed we needed money for TV. He was the manager, and I couldn't micro-manage everything. And then he started putting up the signs early, which I also didn't agree to. And then when I read they violated some ordinance I think, "Great, this is something I didn't want to do and now we're in trouble for it."

So I'm kind of upset. But then I got to thinking about it. What do you mean they have a city ordinance where you can't put up a yard sign? It's a free speech issue, and I taught media law, and had represented The News-Sentinel and clearly, individual property, if not city right-of-way, is where people can put up any sign they want.

We started to take the position with the Moses administration we have a right to put up yard signs in our supporters' yards. And it escalated. We wound up dealing with the right-of-way department, neighborhood code enforcement officials, and these letters back and forth wound up being publicized in the media.

Finally, the issue was making its way to Win and his attorney, Bruce Boxberger. And it was Teetor's advice come true: We had to find a way to engage Moses and get my name out there. And here was an issue we hadn't planned on, yet it fell right in our lap when it came to publicity. I don't think Win's people saw it as a problem: "Here's a city ordinance. Follow it."

But we saw the free speech implications. It being a quiet summer with not a lot of news to cover, TV people covered the issue by focusing on our nice, light blue yard signs. And during neighborhood walks, people began to tell me they had seen my TV ads. However, I hadn't done any new ones since the first ads came out earlier. So, people were seeing the news stories about the yard sign controversy without paying close attention to the fact it wasn't a campaign ad. Yet for the entire month of July, that's exactly what it became.

The controversy develops; we file a lawsuit to overturn the matter. The city finally saw it was hurting Moses politically, so officials wound up settling the case with us. That month, it really helped increase my name ID and gave us an issue that resonated with the average voter.

## Trouble's a-brewing

In August, Win's troubles started to accelerate. The Frank Hopkins trial had started in the murder of neighborhood activist Sharon Lapp. And I'm not sure anyone knew the trial's effect on the city race. But it had a negative effect on Win.

It was the side issues, the ones about how the Police Department was run; about Dave Riemen, the police chief, and Win, showing up at the murder scene afterward and files being removed. And this scenario got into whether Sharon Lapp had some dirt about Moses and his family included in a newsletter from the neighborhood. The case raised the issue of police procedures and Win's role in it.

There were newspaper headlines: "I Smoked Dope in the Mayor's House." Those headlines sure didn't help. And they raised questions about Moses, and even messy police revelations that led to the resignation of Riemen and Public Safety Director Larry Consalvos for their roles in the matter.

Most of the discussion about how to use this information concerned the fact we didn't know when things were going to come up and what would become public from the trial. Our attitude was let's keep our mouths shut and see what happens. Trials aren't political and shouldn't be politicized, even though others might have thought that way. But clearly the fact the trial went on that summer helped us politically because it revealed so much of the details from these sideline issues.

The resignations of Riemen and Consalvos were a sign this wasn't just a legal issue about murder for the public. And it wasn't about somebody just trying to score political points. Instead, there were real problems that led to the resignations. And by coming to a head at this stage, it hurt Moses significantly.

It was the blow that brought us even, and polls after Labor Day had us right around there. But we believed we were still behind because Moses had the money and the recognition.

Then the issue of debates came up. With his weakening politically because of the Lapp case, Win opted to agree to several.

The whole Lapp case tied into how honest was the whole operation. The basic line on Win was always he was a good mayor when it comes to economic development, he was good rallying the community in times of crisis, and he was a bright person. But there was a sense of something shady. His pleading guilty to three misdemeanors to campaign finance violations and the subsequent short-lived resignation were seen as proof of a problem. But again, he was very popular when he returned to office after a Democratic Party caucus vote returned him there after his resignation. I had the sense folks resented him more for coming back after the resignation than the campaign violation charges.

The resentment expanded to how they did the budget, how they did deals, and how they operated the Police Department. People are cynical and questioning of politicians. But it's one thing when it's campaign law or some other relatively arcane issue, another when it gets into police issues where people are very concerned and interested.

**Win the politician**

Because of Win's skill as a politician, the challenge for me was to prove myself. Meanwhile, from Win's perspective, he had to show he was the expert.

I was always impressed with how good Win really is. I know a lot of politicians, and Win is one of the best. Again, he might be lying through his teeth; he might be making it all up. But when he stands in front of a crowd, he knows how to connect with them, he has the right amount of enthusiasm, he says things people want to hear, he tries to tear down and poke holes deftly with the right amount of knife. He's good.

In my time with Win over the years, whenever we're on the same platform, I come away saying to myself, "That guy's good. I'm glad I out got out of there in the 1987 election with a win, because he's tough."

Even when I ran against Evan Bayh in 1998 for U.S. Senate—and Bayh is good—I believe Win's better. In debates with Bayh, he was more of a guy with a good set piece who knew what the script would be and who would try to stay calm and deliver it.

Win could do that as well. But if an unknown came up, whether it was a question from the audience, or someone jumping at him from an angle, Win could handle the situation just about as well as anybody. And I'm not sure Bayh has those skills. He's good. But Win, in terms of his political skills, is tops.

That's why it's so amazing that everything went wrong for him—and some things were out of his control—when things played out in 1987.

**Debating the man**

I felt I was his equal intellectually. But he knew more about city government than I, and he had a lot more experience than I. That's why the first debate was so crucial. Win's attitude was he was going to blow me out of the water at a free-form debate at the Performing Arts Center with questions from the audience after opening statements. Those are the scariest types, because you don't know what they come up with to blindside you. You have to be ready for anything.

We wanted to make sure we had a crowd there because we knew Win would have his supporters from the City-County Building on his side. Dan Heath organized a reception in the gallery beforehand, which brought people out there early. It helped psychologically knowing you have friends out there; even if you're going to screw up, they would clap and bolster you.

Win comes in and his first move is to take off his jacket, loosen his tie, roll up his sleeves. It's one of these psyche moves on your opponents, to show he's the hard-working mayor who knows what he's doing and that he can take care of things. It was the image of the debate being a minor distraction from a busy schedule.

But I wasn't going to change my way. I stayed at the podium, and when the questions came, I answered them well.

I tried to hit my points that we want to do government well, and do finances and police as well. I wasn't rattled.

After the debate, the media and folks in the business community saw me as a legitimate candidate who could do a legitimate job as mayor. It was the crucial thing to get across; I had to show I was a legitimate candidate.

There was a another debate at the chamber; Win realized after the first debate it was going to be tougher this time around.

**Looking the part**

I was coached to this extent: I was helped to look mayoral. I did a faux State of the City speech, and it was taped. And I delivered the speech sitting behind a desk, getting across my themes. As far as preparation for the debates, we at one time had someone ask questions but nobody played the role of Moses. Instead, the idea was just to see how I'd answer potential questions.

I don't do much debate preparation; if you have a free-for-all format, preparation can give you a sense of how you'll answer questions to keep answers short. But sometimes you over-prepare for these things and you never quite sound right. I guess it's just my debate style, a living-on-the-edge kind of feeling.

**Negative campaigning?**

At this stage, the campaign and debates are doing well. We're close and maybe even ahead in the polls. It was great having two newspaper polls because we didn't have the money for our own.

We had to decide toward the end what kind of ads to run after our positive, this-is-Paul-Helmke message. And there was a concern whether Moses would go negative on us and if we should respond.

We prepared a negative ad against Moses, which I thought was very well-done, but it never ran. One of the big issues was whether to run it or not. It was a debate whether to go negative, and I never really liked negative ads and voters don't like them.

The ad reminded people of Moses' legal problems with his campaign finance violations. It showed just the newspaper headlines leading up to Moses' indictment, his response of it as just politics, then onto the "Moses Guilty" headline. No voice-over, except maybe a reading of the headlines leading to the guilty one. And in the end, the ad showed a gavel coming down with "Enough is enough" as the message. For a negative piece, it was well done but I didn't run it.

The Republican state chairman at the time, Gordon Durnil, came down, viewed it and said to run it. A lot of party officials felt the same way.

I made the call not to. I made a point of running a positive campaign and there had been a lot of negatives through allegations in the Lapp trial, about Moses and his brother, but I hadn't been a part of any of it. And I didn't want to be any part of it. I felt I had established credentials on my own, and wanted the folks' emphasis to be on who I was. And if folks had negative feelings about Win, I wanted them to get those feelings on their own and we didn't need to do anything to remind them of it.

## What a strange trip

It was a strange election season. Also with the Lapp case was all the Michael Moses stuff that came up, with him being mentioned as a suspect in the murder of a cleaning woman. I never did understand that. I wasn't involved in any of this stuff. Other folks that might have known from the prosecutor's office what was going on purposely kept me out of it. You can't figure out what everyone is doing or why.

From what I heard, it sounded like officials were doing things legitimately; that there were suspicions in regard to Michael Moses. And if the tip sheet had been publicized, maybe they would have had something. I don't know, I wasn't hearing too much more than the public was.

Apparently, there were a lot of people who hated Win Moses. And they were out to get him and do him in. I obviously had my concerns about Win but I didn't want to be a part of it and wasn't a part of it. Every now and then I heard something was going to happen, "but we're not going to tell you. It might be at the prosecutor's office or someplace else. Just don't ask."

You want to make sure people are playing fair but you don't have a right to find out things from the prosecutor's office.

It was a funny campaign.

## Theories and timing

I didn't believe events were being orchestrated behind the scenes. After I was elected, I went to this new mayor's school put on at Harvard University by the U.S. Conference of Mayors and Harvard's John F. Kennedy School of Government. And each of us had to sum up ourselves, and I summed up a little bit about the election. I told them I ran against a two-term incumbent who had gotten 74 percent of the vote the last time, who had gotten national attention for turning back the flood and

turning around the economy, who had been talked about as a gubernatorial candidate, who had all these political skills, who had an approval rating in April of 65 percent-70 percent, who polls showed led me by 2-1 at
the start of the campaign with the economy going strong. And people
would ask, "How did you ever beat this guy?"

And then, I'd say, at the same time this guy pleaded guilty to three misdemeanors, resigned from office and put himself back in through the precinct
committee people he controlled. He had made headlines about kids smoking dope at the mayor's house, the police chief and safety director resigned,
and his brother is accused of murder. And they said, "Why didn't you wipe
this guy out?"

It was timing that wasn't orchestrated. These events, starting with the yard
signs and then the Lapp trial and the Michael Moses situation, they just
all fell into place. There are people who believe in conspiracy theories;
instead, I've always believed things sometimes just happen. It's occurred to
me before, if not for the yard signs, the Lapp case wouldn't have had the
same effect because I'd be seen as someone who really wasn't contesting
Win, so the situation surrounding her murder was no big deal.

### Day of reckoning

It was all a blur on Election Day, but I still believed Win was going to win.
He had a lot of positives going for him, despite taking a lot of hits.

Come Election Day, it's like 70 degrees and sunny, and I ponder the old
standard line about good weather helping Democrats. Oh boy, this isn't
going to help at all.

A lot of my tactics were to focus on Democratic parts of town. My theory was to run everywhere; I'd walk Democrat, swing and GOP districts.
And near the end, I focused more on Democrat and swing districts. With
research, I found some precincts where a Democrat would win like 350-
10. There were some precincts where Republicans wouldn't even get into

double figures. Popular political wisdom says don't even campaign there, you'll get wiped out anyway. My theory is you try to campaign everywhere, and I spent a lot of time in those precincts. It paid off for me; I still lost those precincts, but instead of by 350-10 I lost them 150-20, for example. It might sound like a wipeout but there's a difference of a couple hundred votes from past GOP showings.

It's election night and people are at the house. I'm getting excited; I have a scotch or two. But I don't want to drink too much because I'll have to speak later. But I'm also nervous and when some of the returns from my home precinct come in, I realize it's close.

And then around 9 p.m., Win comes on the television and concedes. I was shocked. Someone asked me after the election when I had thought I would win. And I said I didn't believe I had it won until he conceded because he knew more about these things than I did. I went downtown; the place is packed at the Summit Club. What an exciting night! I won by about 2,200 votes. All of a sudden the reality hits me. "I won this thing."

I felt I could handle it fine; this is what I prepared for all my life, government and politics. I looked at it a little bit like an outsider, like "Hmm, this is interesting. I'm going to do this now." It's a real challenge; it's such an important job. You don't realize how complicated the job is when you first run; you really do after you perform the job. It shows the limits of what you can do.

The next morning also is great, but all of a sudden you realize you have to put all this together and the headaches come soon enough. You realize a lot of the campaign was an anti-Moses vote. So the challenge for me was how to become not the anti-Moses but my own person. It's a challenge when voters unite to get somebody; it's hard to get those voters to support the winner as well.

On election night I went to the Fraternal Order of Police, where a lot of police officers had supported me, and they were rowdy and boisterous in celebration. And I said to myself, these are a lot of officers who wanted Chief Riemen and Moses out. But now, they all want to be police chief. And once I start picking and saying it's going to be this person and not these others, those officers aren't going to be too happy.

You figure quickly it's easier to campaign against somebody than to put together a coalition of your own.

### Getting started

A lot of it, however, was fairly easy. Dan Heath stayed as chief of staff. My friend and law firm partner Tim McCaulay became city attorney. Linda Buskirk and John Stafford, who were involved in the campaign, were asked to come aboard. A lot of the people I identified during the campaign as good people I knew I would want to have stay on.

I wanted to keep somebody from the Moses administration to show we were going to be inclusive and weren't just going to throw out all the old folks. We ended up keeping Greg Purcell, from community and economic development. Despite him being a controversial official chosen originally by Moses, it turned out to be one of the better decisions I made. And I really didn't know Purcell that well.

Police chief was the hardest choice to make. I wanted to make sure we had a good selection to choose from. A lot of names were floated around; Greg Lewis had worked on the campaign and his name was mentioned, so were Neil Moore's and Dan Hannaford's. I'd go to police officers and ask for their pluses and minuses about these candidates, and Neil's came up positive the most. It surprised me; he hadn't worked on the campaign and I really didn't know him. It was down to Hannaford and Moore, and Neil had a bit of an edge on Hannaford, so I chose him as chief and Hannaford as assistant chief.

## Nothing quite like it

I've always had a healthy ego and I think highly of my skills; I think that way whether I'm winning or losing. But winning is nice.

The challenge is not to allow the adulation and praise change the way you think of yourself or the way you do things. And I don't think it did. I've never been shy about liking attention and liking to be paid attention to; I like it whether I'm in office or not. But it sure didn't hurt.

If someone's looking for a thrill or a real high, winning, especially when you're the underdog, is one of the highest highs you can get. It feels great.

## Cast of characters:

**Ed Rousseau**—Allen County commissioner; also elected to the City Council and Allen County Council

**Orvas Beers**—Former long-time chairman of the Allen County Republican Party

**Alan McMahan**—Former city chairman of the Allen County Republican Party

**Dan Heath**—Now an Allen Superior Court judge, Heath served as Helmke's campaign manager and chief adviser; lost to Jill Long for 4th District U.S. Representative in 1989

**Frank Hopkins**—Convicted of the May, 1985 stabbing death of neighborhood activist Sharon Lapp

**Sharon Lapp**—Neighborhood activist found murdered in her south-side home; kept files of alleged wrongdoing by city officials in the Moses administration

**Moses' Police Chief David Riemen and Public Safety Director Larry Consalvos**—Both stepped down for their involvement in the mishandling of evidence in the Lapp murder investigation

**Michael Moses**—Win Moses' brother, who was mentioned as a suspect in the 1987 murder of a dentist office cleaning woman; no charges were ever brought against him

# WELCOME TO THE SUMMIT CITY, YOU'VE BEEN ANNEXED

*Photo by Ellie Bogue*

**Message in a box**

During controversy over annexing the Adams Center landfill, a white Cheddar and spinach pizza that Mayor Paul Helmke picked up from the Munchie Emporium contained a not-so-subliminal hypnotic message that an employee had written inside the pizza box. "I am getting sleepy. My eyelids are getting heavy. I am falling into a trance. I will oppose expansion of the landfill. I am getting sleepy. I will do all in my power to protect the safety of the citizens of Fort Wayne regardless of income level. I am falling into a deep trance. I will not compromise the future health of future generations. I do not want the pizza maker to be upset with me. I am getting sleepy. Boy, this was a great pizza." A bemused Helmke kept the pizza box top.

Annexation has always interested me.

Growing up around State and Anthony boulevards, I saw what the community was evolving into. For example, my mother's family lived on West Drive, and the area just to the north of it was farmland. Kirkwood Park was not that much farther away, yet it was outside the city limits, even when I was starting high school.

I sensed growing up here how things changed and how things grew. For a kid who lived on the north side of town, Time Corners on the southwest side was the end of the universe. In the eighth grade, I had a crush on this girl in my class who lived in the Glenwood neighborhood. I remember riding my bike to Glenwood. Not only was it a huge distance, but you rode past this farm field on State and Lake avenues to get there. It was one of those new suburbs very far out there.

When I attended North Side High School, the area from where students came from was large. It took in most of St. Joe Township. A part of Fort Wayne Community Schools was even outside the city limits. So when you went on dates or parties with students from such faraway neighborhoods as Waterswolde or Hacienda Village, you realized how much farmland you were driving past to get there.

After law school, I saw how much the town had grown up. It became urbanized. You really got the sense what was once farmland was now truly urban and part of the city. I used to mention Devils Hollow; it was just a place kids went to park with their girlfriends. It was just an isolated area way out there in horse country. It was something different then and the nature of it has changed in the last 20-30 years.

It also was interesting to see housing and commercial patterns change. Even before I was paying too much attention, the stores downtown like Sears moved to Rudisill Boulevard when I started kindergarten in 1954. It was after I graduated from high school that Glenbrook Square opened up. You saw these changing patterns. The people who lived on my street or went to my school were moving out.

**An early interest**

So when I started out as a young lawyer, I became active with Fort Wayne Future. And one of the topics I got interested in was government structure and annexation. I can still remember John Stafford, a young planner with the city, speaking to us about what had happened with annexation in Indianapolis and Lexington, Ky. We talked about the different outcomes that could occur in a community with annexation. And if a city didn't annex in ways that reflected growth and demographic and economic realities, a community needed to look at a new structure of government.

I got involved also in the early 1980s doing legal work for the St. Joe Township community association in its fight with the private utility Inbalco, the predecessor of Utility Center, now AquaSource. Folks were getting crummy water from the private utility. It looked like orange Faygo pop. We had a lot of battles with state regulatory groups to pay attention.

Eventually, we raised the issue to such a profile, the city came in and acquired that portion of the utility with the goal of providing quality water for suburban homeowners.

I still remember talks with the township association at the time when the city, with Win Moses Jr. as mayor, made annexation overtures. People said if the city asks for annexation in return for good water, they would do it. Then, the city bought the private utility system in St. Joe, gave residents good water and never asked them to be annexed. It struck me as a missed opportunity. While I was happy for my clients who got good water, I wondered why annexation discussions weren't occurring at the same time.

In 1983, when Bud Meeks was running against Moses for mayor, I worked on that campaign and researched the issue of annexation. There was some sense that a number of annexations that were started under the previous administration of Republican Mayor Bob Armstrong were not advancing. Other than an attempt to take in the Blackhawk neighborhood, which was languishing in court, not much else was happening.

**An election issue**

Then, when I decided to run in 1987, one of the points I made from the start was the fact we had not been aggressive enough in annexation and had fallen behind. The inactivity was hurting the long-term future of the community. And I sensed at the time, annexation wasn't happening for political considerations. A Democratic city administration and City Council might be reluctant to annex areas seen as Republican.

Regardless of politics, annexation was important. While Moses was not against annexation, Democrats paid lip service to it. But I made it a top priority. I wanted to go after all adjacent areas that hadn't been incorporated. For example, I was for taking in the area between Fort Wayne and New Haven. The fight over those East End industries had been languishing since the early 1950s. It just didn't make sense to me.

When I got into office, I made it clear to officials that annexation was a top priority. We formed an annexation team not only of planners, but also legal staff, advisers, and service providers. We kept it in place throughout my 12 years. We discussed pending annexations, litigation and legislation on annexation.

One of the early discussions centered on where would we start. Northeast was the obvious choice. It was the most urbanized and urbanized the longest. It had gotten larger since the late 1950s, when the Nickel Plate railroad was elevated downtown to eliminate train crossing delays. As a result, it opened up migration to the suburbs. No longer was the north side of town the area of State and Anthony boulevards.

## The county isn't the answer

Earlier, as assistant county attorney, I had worked for the county highway department. One of the testy issues dealt with Arlington Park, outside the city. Residents had raised issues about maintenance of streets and curbs. The highway department's philosophy was it didn't handle residential neighborhoods, or its streets and curbs. Instead, it maintained county line roads and long thoroughfares. It dawned on me that county government was not set up to deal with these issues. The services Arlington Park wanted were the kind the city could provide. My 14-year experience with county government showed it wasn't set up to deal with urbanized issues. Instead, the county was better off dealing with rural and less dense parts of town.

When we chose to annex northeast, we made several significant decisions. One was tactical. We'd go after big areas instead of a small. In the past, annexations were small and incremental. The last large annexations were of Canterbury Green and Glenbrook Square. Since then, they were of smaller areas like the Blackhawk and Marketplace of Canterbury neighborhoods. Yet we noticed the city faced the same amount of delays, legal fights and citizen anger from a small annexation as from a large one. If the city was going to have annexations languish in courts and pay lawyers to pursue them, you might as well go for a big chunk. It costs you about the same in terms of time and controversy.

## A phased approach

Another significant decision was to structure the northeast annexation into four phases. It became one large annexation, portions of which came in at different times. It appeared people would be less angry the longer you waited before actually taking them in. The longer it took for the extra taxes through annexation to kick in, the less likely people would be willing to pay money to fight the takeover.

Using deferral dates made a lot of sense. Without them, it was easy for opponents to get contributions from property owners. A court battle would allow people in an area to delay annexation, and the longer they stalled, the more those people were saving in taxes as opposed to being brought in right away.

But with a three-year deferral, arguments from opponents made a lot less sense. If the issue was settled during that time, all you've done is paid for lawyers without any savings in return. We used deferrals as a tactic to win and to better plan the delivery of services in large areas. We just weren't sure how the strategy would hold up in court.

## An uncertain future

Would people fight it? Would City Council go along? How would the courts respond? If this didn't work, then we should focus on consolidating local government. If annexation wasn't going to work, we'd argue consolidation was the only way to effectively deal with sprawl, growth and a shrinking tax base. But if annexation worked, we hoped suburban folks would realize they'd eventually become a part of the city, so why pay city and county taxes? Why have the duplication and overlap of government?

We had a law on the books for annexation, but not for creating a consolidated, unigov-like government. So we opted to try annexation as a tactic first, even though both issues were somewhat interchangeable.

We also tried to take care of our pending annexation in Blackhawk. It had languished so long in court we dismissed it and started again. The same with the Tamarack neighborhood. We met with Mayor Lynn Shaw to resolve the New Haven issue as well. We decided which areas New Haven would annex, and those Fort Wayne would take. We now border each other.

We spent a lot of time putting together a good plan, announced it at the end of 1988 and scheduled public hearings.

One of the biggest mistakes was a slip of the tongue from Greg Purcell, than head of Community and Economic Development. We had a major meeting scheduled in December to discuss annexation with residents. We set up the meeting as non-confrontational as possible. Instead of a mayor facing an angry crowd, we set up the meeting in a high school gym with different tables for people to get answers about services, like police and fire protection. Officials were there to answer questions, not to provide a forum for anti-annexation supporters.

But the first meeting happened on a poor weather night. Purcell gets quoted the next day saying the poor turnout showed people in St. Joe must support annexation. My reaction? Oh, don't say things like that! It's like a team putting up on a blackboard a controversial saying from an opposing player to get the blood boiling. The quote got people stirred up. And I mean they really got stirred up.

### Angry folks in St. Joe

In a lot of ways, St. Joe was a lot more bitter and controversial than the annexation effort in Aboite Township. People were angry. When the City Council had a hearing, people packed the room with signs: "King

Helmke's Tax" and "It Ain't Over Till the Fat Lady Sings!" were some of the nastier ones.

Part of the timing was interesting. Annexation was coming up the same time there was another City Council vote coming up on creating a local income tax. And, there was the special election to fills Dan Coats seat in Congress when he went to the Senate after Dan Quayle became George Bush's vice president. I decided not to run for Congress so as not to politicize the issues of the county option income tax or annexation. I realized both of votes would be on a party line if the issues became politicized. And with City Council 7-2 Democrat, I knew I'd lose both on the tax and annexation issues.

But I got support from the council on annexation, even from hard-liners like Councilman and former mayor Paul Mike Burns.

During the special election for Congress, Jill Long used these issues against Dan Heath, my chief of staff and her opponents. She criticized him for being part of an administration that pushed these controversial and disliked issues. Yet there was no response from the Heath for Congress staff to these accusations. Instead, St. Joe residents put up tables next to polling places on Election Day to collect petition signatures against the annexation. Eventually, St. Joe residents turned in what appeared to be enough signatures. But some were eventually thrown out as invalid, lowering the number to less than half required by law to mount a successful court challenge to annexation.

### You can't make everyone happy

I've been criticized in the most recent Aboite annexation for not working with folks out there. But one of the lessons from St. Joe is you can work with every group you find to make them happy, but there's always another group that isn't. Nobody really speaks for the group as a whole or can act for the whole until you have litigation that brings the two sides to court.

We had separate discussions with Hacienda Village and Arlington Park about improvements out there; we tried to reach agreement with them. We also met about Fire Department issues. Folks liked the township volunteer fire department. So we tried to work with the township trustee and fire department, and reached an agreement we believed fair regarding a dual fire response and hiring some of their people.

Seemed like a reasonable effort people were asking for. Instead, elected folks from St. Joe who cut the deal were seen as trafficking with the enemy and were thrown out. Ken Nicolet is now the street commissioner, and Jack Webb, from the board, came on to work for the city after they in effect were thrown out politically for daring to even speak with us.

It became a more strident group, and it got testier as the battle lines were drawn. When we went to court, we believed there were enough signatures we could dispute as invalid to bring opponents under a 50 percent majority, squashing the lawsuit. It all depended on how you counted the signatures and how you considered sewer waivers, multiple property owners, and husband and wife signatures. We lost at the trial court level, as we have in the Aboite annexation. But we won reversal on appeal, and as a result, won the case with a final decision in September 1991.

### It's all in the timing

I felt good about the timing. We moved this thing through in about two years. This one didn't languish in court forever. The bad part, however, was the decision came about two months before I'm running for re-election for the first time against Democrat Charlie Belch. And all the while, the city has added new voters with "King Helmke's Tax" and "It Ain't Over Till the Fat Lady Sings" signs in their yards. I wasn't sure how it would affect me politically. But I carried nearly all the precincts, although by lesser Republican margins than in the past. My take on the results? While annexation was controversial, there was a difference between controversial and popular. The people who were very vocal and loud were not the majority. The lesson I learned is you're not hearing from the majority of the people. Instead, you're hearing just from the people who want to be loud.

However, there never was a legal challenge to the use of a phased-in strategy of annexation because the matter was lost when opponents failed to get enough signatures for a lawsuit. The annexation was never judged on its merits, including the use of phases. We never were sure what would have happened if the courts had ruled on the merits, But when it comes to annexation, cities usually win on the merits. We had done our homework, especially with service delivery.

### So what's all the fuss?

When the whole thing ended, annexation didn't have any major negative political impact and in St. Joe, there were no further legal challenges.

I still talk with Stafford and others, and they're amazed we pulled it off. We put a lot of eggs in this one basket and no one was sure if it would hold up politically or legally, and if we could get it done. But we got it done.

And it's worked well. We've now brought in all four phases. We're providing the services we promised even though some folks are still disgruntled. We've added fire stations, increased city personnel and are doing a good job.

### Let's be fair

Here's an example I give people when speaking of the need for annexation:

At one stage in the St. Joe annexation battle, there was a controversy in the Blackhawk area about crossing guards and stoplights on State Boulevard near Blackhawk school. Children who were going to the middle school from the north had to cross State. The area was outside the city limits at the time. Residents were lobbying county commissioners for a light or something else to make it safer. Commissioner Ed Rousseau even went out there and acted as a crossing guard to get a sense of the problem. But the county wasn't sure how much it would cost and if it could afford the project.

Finally, somebody from the parents group realized if they targeted the effort a block to the west, they'd be right on the city boundary line. The city boundary line at that time came up to a sharp point, like a point on a square, at the intersection of State and Arrowhead Drive. People realized the intersection was right there on the city limits. They argued to me the city should put in a stoplight to deal with safety concerns in the vicinity. And folks raised a lot of legitimate issues.

We brought the people in for a meeting in my conference room. We had a blown-up map of the area. After I heard their pitch, I said, let me get this straight. Blackhawk Middle School where these kids are going to, isn't the school outside the city limits? Yes, it's in Fort Wayne Community Schools but outside the city limits. Hmm. Now, the kids that have to dodge the cars, are they in the city limits? Well, all these kids were in the Blackhawk neighborhood north of State so they lived outside the city limits. Meanwhile, kids who lived south of State and west of Arrowhead were inside the city limits, and didn't have to cross the street.

School's outside the city, kids are outside the city, but we must be concerned about them. Well, it costs about $40,000 for a light, and to get the light hooked up to the traffic computer. With the kids and school outside the city limits, I'm trying to figure out justification for spending $40,000 of city taxpayer money for the project. So I asked about these cars the kids are dodging. We actually had done a study. These cars are going both ways. With morning traffic, 80 percent is coming from outside the city to Fort Wayne to work when kids are going to school. In the evening, it's the opposite, people heading for the suburbs to go home.

So you're asking me to spend city money for kids who live outside the city, who go to a school outside the city, who dodge cars from outside the city.

What's the fairness of this? I have citizens in the city with unmet needs that still want traffic lights like this.

Their response was, "Oh, we don't want to talk about annexation. We don't want to get into those controversial political issues. We're talking about the safety of our kids." And I said that's precisely the point. I'm concerned about the safety of your kids too. Annexation is an issue because it gets into how and who provides services. It was clear from the discussion the artificial boundary at that point made no sense. And I tried to get the point across.

## The poor subsidizing the rich

I wasn't done; I asked another question to figure out the justification. Maybe this is a poor neighborhood. We had done some studies and found out neighborhoods outside the city have an income of $35,000 a household; a household inside the city, $25,000. So not only was the traffic light for a school outside the city, for kids outside the city, dodging cars outside the city, suburban residents are asking the poorer part of the population to pay for it while they, the wealthier residents, don't.

I asked one last question. Maybe there was a special circumstance about the Blackhawk area. The only special circumstance I could find is the fact for the last 12 years Blackhawk residents were paying an attorney to fight us from making them a part of the city.

Again, this just shows how artificial boundary lines need to reflect where people live and work. The traffic light issue brought home the need for annexation and how you equitably pay for services. It's a question of trying to make sense of this nonsense.

## A matter of class

To me it's a class issue. It's why long-range annexation makes sense. The older parts of a city are generally going to have a higher level of poverty, more senior citizens and most likely, a declining tax base. Businesses move to the malls at the edge of the city, affluent young families move to the suburbs and sometimes what follows are demolitions and patterns of urban decay. There are more minorities in the central city as well. If you don't move the artificial boundary lines to reflect where people are living, then you're going to get more pronounced inequities as to who is asked to pay for services.

Everyone benefits from a strong central city because of work, jobs, shopping and culture. Folks choosing a site for a new business often look at the downtown even if they are planning to locate in a cornfield in the suburbs because it shows how a community is taking care of itself. I've always made the point the challenges of crime, unemployment, blizzards and floods don't stop at the city limits. And the opportunities for growth don't stop there either. You got to have this kind of growth. If you can't have consolidated government to erase political boundary lines altogether, then actual boundary lines should reflect economic and demographic reality.

With the concept of unigov, I have always said you don't have to tax all people at the same rate. Urban and rural areas can be charged differently because of differing needs. You can have a single government and service providers but a two-tiered tax rate, like in Lexington, Ky. The most logical way would be to make it a function of planning. When land changes from cornfields to homes and businesses, then the territory changes its tax category from rural to urban. It would make boundary line decisions not controversial and political, but a land planning solution.

## The hypocrisy of it all

I'm ticked off about the inherent hypocrisy. I've made the same arguments about annexation and consolidated government for 14 years. It's frustrating. There are so many misconceptions and untruths. You are always going to fight this battle. On this one, I've always been right, I've always been consistent and I feel like I'm going to keep saying the same thing about it. It's the one issue I really care about.

Annexation points out the inherent unfairness. It's a class issue. It's a racial issue. Part of it you see as the snobbery. Part of it you see as short-term thinking. If the only focus is what's my tax bill going to be next year, I can see why people oppose it. If you see it in terms of what's life going to be like for my kids and me the next 20 years and beyond, than you get a different response.

As someone who grew up here and whose family is from Fort Wayne, I see Fort Wayne in the long-term context. I would hope others who are living here could see it that way too. When you think long term about a community, whether your next year's tax bill goes up 30 percent or not isn't as important as whether the community is able to deal with its needs in the long run. That's a hard thing to get through to people and businesses.

**They don't want higher taxes**

Part of what bugs me is the complaint about how high people's taxes will become with annexation. Well, when an area's annexed, residents end up paying the same as I've been paying as a city resident all my life. And it's the same for others who live on Pontiac Street, Forest Park Boulevard or in Southwood Park. You get the impression Aboite Township is going to get saddled with brand-new, heavy taxes. Well, these are new taxes to them but they are the ones city residents have paid forever. If somehow I've been able to handle it, my neighbors have been able to handle it, why can't they handle it? They should be able to. It's the point I keep trying to make.

One of the advantages of Fort Wayne is the fact we haven't been hemmed in by old neighbors. You don't bump into older historic neighborhoods right on the border. In Aboite Township, the so-called towns of West Hamilton or Aboite aren't independent communities. Leo and Grabill, Monroeville and Huntertown are, not Aboite. There wasn't anything in St.

Joe Township either. These areas don't have a history as individual towns. It's a tricky situation when the city's trying to grow, for example, and it bumps up against Leo. Even trickier was when the city bumped into Waynedale in the 1950s, because the area had a separate identity.

## Smaller isn't always better

I get into arguments with folks that Republicans stand for less government, support a return of power home and the belief smaller is always better. But smaller is not always better. There are some issues to be dealt with on the local, not state or national, level. But often it's not the most efficient way to fix the streets, hire police, or deal with water and sewer services. You have to decide what should be the size to effectively deal with urban issues. Township government, for example, is not inherently better because it's smaller. Most folks don't even know what their township is, who's their township trustee and who serves on the advisory board. They don't know the township's budget and where the money goes.

People focus all the time on the income taxes I've passed. Yet these townships gets some of that income tax revenue. Does anybody know what they spend it on? You know what the city spends it on, or at least we try to publicize it. Some issues can be handled on the neighborhood level, but they are often connected to a larger picture.

It's where annexation and government consolidation come in: They are attempts to find out the right size to deal with issues. Things have changed a lot in 150 years. Fort Wayne is the capital of northeast Indiana. Folks in Angola and LaGrange come here to shop. It's not an argument for annexing those areas. But it's an argument for looking at the reality of how the economy works, how transportation patterns have evolved, and figuring out how to set up government. Local governmental has to change as technology, housing and demographic patterns change.

## Holding a grudge against me

How did people personalize it against me? I used to joke that whenever a safety issue was brought up, I said I felt safe almost anywhere except in St. Joe. We tried to win people over during neighborhood walks after annexation, and sometimes it got a bit testy.

When you talk with people one-on-one, this is their attitude: We don't want to be annexed, we don't want to pay higher taxes, but we knew it was coming. I had so many people tell me that when they finally got city water, they knew annexation would follow. I had people who moved to the suburbs tell me the real estate agent made it known the area would be annexed in two or three years.

Maybe annexation wasn't their favorite thing, but they were blind if they didn't see it coming. Actually, most of them believed it was coming 10-20 years earlier, and were fortunate enough to get an extra 10-20 years of freedom they weren't counting on. People realized they were part of the Fort Wayne community and, as a result, annexation was the right thing to do.

I'd get nasty messages at home. I get folks who continue to do that. But when I had a chance to explain my point of view, even with those who'd disagree with me, they'd realize it was being done for strong legitimate reasons.

Politically, I kept thinking since I'm catching flak from these areas I'm annexing, I ought to be getting countervailing support from the people already in Fort Wayne. But that's politics: People against something get more revved up and hot than those who are supportive.

## It helps city taxpayers

I tried to get the argument across to city neighborhoods that annexation is helping them in the pocketbook. While speaking with Memorial Park neighborhood residents, the issues they brought up were housing and the park pool. But I told them annexation is important as well for these reasons:

If suburbanites pay higher taxes, it means they are helping keep your taxes low, and providing you with better streets, stronger police and better economic development. A lot of folks never made the connection. I still see letters to the editor saying the city shouldn't annex new areas because Fort Wayne should be taking care of what it has now.

But a reason we can't take care of what we have now is because the city has fallen behind on annexation. Meanwhile, annexation allows us to pay for services more equitably, deliver services more efficiently and keep taxes low. Part of keeping property taxes low was passage of the income tax; part of it was revenue from annexation. They allowed us to keep taxes low and help neighborhoods.

The reason Aboite and St. Joe fights annexation is the reason every city neighborhood should be enthusiastically for it.

**Political suicide**

Was I helping the GOP while screwing myself politically? It occurred to me that might be happening. We got more Republican voters with annexation while I'm doing political damage to myself. But I tried to present annexation as a nonpartisan issue. Council was Democratic, yet it approved annexation. I have to salute City Council members. The entire time I was mayor, the council looked at annexation as good for the city, not whether it was bringing in Republicans or something bad for Democrats. And that's how it should be.

Yes, it struck me that while I'm making all these folks really angry and committing political suicide, I'm helping the local Republican Party in the long run. I'm not the sort to sacrifice myself for the good of the Republican Party. But it was the right thing to do for the city. If anything, I wish Republicans would have given me a little more credit for helping them out.

My tactics were always pretty clear as to major annexations. I would do a major annexation at the start of each term. Pine Valley in 1992 after my second election, Aboite in 1996 after the third. I was always pretty clear I wanted to get the adjacent urban areas and I would be moving around the city in a counterclockwise way because that's where development occurred first. First St. Joe, then Pine Valley, then Aboite.

Pine Valley, coming in the next two years, wasn't very controversial at all. You never saw the animosity and nastiness like in other areas. Folks there saw we were winning in court and delivering services fairly smoothly. You didn't hear people complain they weren't getting services they had been promised.

I remember going to a St. Joe meeting where someone made a big deal about not getting services promised him. I checked into it and learned the area he was talking about wasn't part of the area that was annexed. And the situation proves a point: People just don't know where is that arbitrary boundary line.

Pine Valley went relatively smoothly and I wished Aboite had gone the same way. Around this time of the Aboite annexation, legislators got involved. None of those legislators, it seemed, wanted to run out and change the law for St. Joe or Pine Valley. But for Aboite, legislators seemed to have a different agenda.

**We also took on a landfill**

The annexation of Adams Center landfill also was controversial, but for different reasons. One, it was voluntary; the landfill wanted to be part of Fort Wayne and not New Haven, its other neighbor. Second, it was part of our battles with New Haven over territory. And third, the existence of a hazardous waste landfill had a lot of opposition in the community even before Fort Wayne annexed it.

I separated the issue of the landfill's desire to expand from the issue of annexing the property. When an area came to me requesting voluntary annexation, I didn't know how I could logically say no at the same time I was aggressively pushing annexation in other areas. This was at a time St. Joe had just ended, and Pine Valley's annexation was getting readied. I had to be consistent. I was going to annex all the adjacent urban areas, or basically, anything I could.

All of a sudden, I'm presented with a case that wasn't on our target list or an area we had been looking at that wanted to come in voluntarily. My first concern was how can I logically say no, I don't want you in the city, even though you're trying to be annexed voluntarily, but say yes when it's not voluntary with anybody else. It's really hard to defend the moral high ground of my philosophy everyone should be part of the city and paying for its future when I was willing to do it with folks who didn't want to come in but not willing to do it with folks who did.

I wasn't just thinking about the landfill, but our long-term strategy for the city. I didn't want it thrown at us we were picking and choosing. If we were accused of that, it would weaken our position, at least politically.

Annexation did not equal expansion, I always said. Other folks wanted to turn it into an issue about what the landfill was doing. That to me was a separate issue.

### David vs. Goliath

Part of the whole discussion also dealt with the situation between New Haven and Fort Wayne situation. Annexation meant we would be competing with New Haven long range. While I wanted New Haven to grow and prosper, I didn't want New Haven to be encroaching on areas I considered part of Fort Wayne or its growth.

Since the first term, we had a number of run-ins with New Haven. On the other side of town, there was the Shordon Estates area. If Fort Wayne had done this kind of annexation, we would have been lambasted by the media. Basically, New Haven went up Landin Road and just annexed the road and then annexed the neighborhood on top of the road. It looks like a little flag atop New Haven's boundary line.

I considered the area north of the river more properly part of Fort Wayne's growth, not New Haven's, it's why Shordon Estates was of such sensitivity to us. I didn't want New Haven moving too much into St. Joe Township or moving down the southeast side of Fort Wayne. New Haven moving east was fine.

Once New Haven started going for the landfill, we got concerned. We wanted to be able to control our future growth and not have New Haven make an end-run around us. We were really concerned about how New Haven was going about its business. New Haven basically annexed the area in a single night. Our procedures for annexation called for a plan commission hearing and a public hearing before City Council. Our process, even on a short time line, still was about three weeks. New Haven announced it, introduced, waived the rules and voted on it all in a single evening. It got us very concerned about how New Haven was doing business. It not only made us nervous, but concerned about anything else New Haven could be up to in adjoining areas.

### Landfill nervous of New Haven

New Haven's actions, however, were thrown out by the court. As a result, the landfill folks came to us requesting voluntary annexation. We checked to make sure we weren't picking up a huge liability. We did some research and found out, because of potential liabilities in the future, many communities got agreements on tipping fees and extra payments from the landfill.

So we asked for some considerations to protect us from future negatives. We reached an agreement on tipping fees, some of which went to the

Central City Housing Trust Fund, and it helped us do quite a bit in southeast Fort Wayne. Some other dollars came in. My attitude is if they want to be annexed, and are willing to pay more for housing and public works for the community, why not? It didn't commit us one way or another to expansion; it's how things worked out in the end.

## Statewide reputation

I developed a statewide reputation on annexation, although I'm not sure it's a good one. As we did more of them, and were moving in a counter-clockwise direction, folks in Aboite knew it was coming. One of the thing folks out there did was work the legislative route more than in the past.

Sometimes we had legislators who believed they were helping the city. But we weren't sure whether they were helping or not. Mitch Harper, for example, used to come up with ideas that at some levels could have helped us but on other levels, could have hurt us as well. After our first year, we realized it was even dangerous to raise the issue of annexation with the Legislature. We were more likely to get anti-annexation language instead of language in the law that could have helped us negotiate with residents about different kinds of municipal services and different ways to pay for them.

## On the defense

So, we went from a proactive position to a more defensive position, particularly when we got closer to the Aboite annexation. We began to hear more anti-annexation rumblings from the state legislature, particularly from Rep. Bob Alderman. It's interesting to note, as long as it was just Rep. Alderman, we were able to keep things from changing against us in the General Assembly.

Things started to get tricky when other legislators supported anti-annexation legislation because of concerns in their communities. One was Rep. Dean Mock from the Elkhart area; often, Alderman would hook up with

Mock and his approach against annexation. Even then, working with the Indiana Association of Cities and Towns, we were pretty effective keeping things from changing. It was one of the benefits from my active participation in IACT; with my involvement, and my becoming its president, IACT folks were lobbied for us along with pro-annexation mayors from other parts of the state.

Things also got really tricky when the city of Carmel started to do aggressive annexation. Carmel is a wealthy area, with a healthy growth rate, north of Indy. It hit home when a new mayor in 1995 began to aggressively annex. It caught the eye of legislators around Indy and they have quite a bit of clout.

### Legislators gang up on us

So we had the Alderman and Mock efforts under control. But when the Indy area legislators got upset about Carmel's activities, it got harder to fight off legislative efforts to change the rules. Eventually, we had a couple of sessions it looked like we were really going to get messed over. And Rep. Win Moses did a great job helping us keep things from changing.

It's interesting. Here's Win, who was my opponent in 1987, who now is a legislator who obviously understood municipal issues. He really did a great job helping the city fight back some of the most extreme anti-annexation legislation. It was fun. At an IACT convention in Fort Wayne afterward, Win was awarded legislator of the year by the association. It felt good to give him the award as thanks for his efforts. It shows in politics you could have folks you run against or are opposed to you on some issues on your side at other times. But you keep the lines of communication open with them nevertheless to work with them on other issues.

The anti-annexation spirit kept growing. We were able to beat back any attempts to make changes retroactive, which would have really hurt us on the Aboite annexation, introduced in late 1996.

## Et tu, David Long?

What also hurt us was state Sen. David Long, who was part of the anti-annexation efforts. The situation was very disappointing to me. Long had been a strong supporter of annexation while on the City Council. He had voted for every annexation ordinance that we had introduced until the summer of 1995. Then, when he had already become a candidate for state Senate, I remember joking with some folks that we had helped him out by passing an annexation ordinance in the summer of 1995. It gave Long an annexation ordinance to vote against to make his anti-annexation conversion look a little bit more honest.

Part of the equation with Long is he believed he'd have a primary election race with Mitch Harper for the open state Senate seat when John Sinks stepped down. Harper had some concerns with annexation law when he had been in the Legislature, had done some things with New Haven, and had been talking about the issue. Long felt he had to establish his bonafide anti-annexation credentials or he'd be in danger in the GOP primary election.

Harper, however, ended up not running but Long had already staked out his position. But at least, Long came across as someone in the state Senate we could talk work with in moderating some of the more strident anti-annexation tendencies. But having Long in the Senate, joining Alderman in the House, combined with other anti-annexation communities statewide made it tougher and tougher to fight the backlash. The Legislature finally did pass some legislation in 1999. But crucial to us was the fact the legislation wasn't retroactive, hurting us in Aboite Township.

The legislation made it harder to annex, but not impossible. It was one of the tactics the Aboite group used more successfully than people in other parts of town. They were able to get their state legislators on board. It strikes me as a bit tricky for some of these legislators to answer questions about why they didn't get involved when some areas were being annexed, but jumped into the fray when Aboite was involved.

## Aboite in Fort Wayne makes sense

The Aboite area is one I believed all along fit the criteria we had been talking about. It was an increasingly urbanized area, clearly tied to the city. It hadn't been an independent entity; people in Aboite had their jobs based in Fort Wayne areas, they were connected to Fort Wayne, their future livelihood depended on Fort Wayne. Fort Wayne's success dealing with crime, public works and economic development directly affected them.

Therefore, it made sense it should come in after St. Joe and Pine Valley. But it also clearly was an area that ought to be part of the city for all the right reasons. There were things we could do to help out the Aboite area. In public works, the area needed a lot with utilities. While not required by an annexation plan, we felt it was something we could offer that could make a difference for residents there. The same was true with traffic issues, whether it meant removing the tracks on West Jefferson near Swinney Park or other long-range issues. We believed the city could help them.

The anti-annexation folks started organizing long before we introduced our plan. I used to hear from attorneys and friends they were getting ready to fight; a lot of folks saw it coming. And we were pushed into doing things even more quickly than I had wanted by legislative efforts and efforts to incorporate into the town of West Hamilton.

It was after the legislative session of 1995, when Alderman had some introduced anti-annexation legislation, where he and I reached an agreement that put the legislation on hold. Meanwhile, I put annexation on hold while we tried to see if things could be worked out.

## Ever heard of West Hamilton?

But after the 1995 session had ended, folks in Aboite went to the County Commissioners, asking to be incorporated as the town of West Hamilton. To me, the move was a real challenge to the future of our community. If we had an incorporated entity of West Hamilton, or any other name out there, it would make annexation impossible and would hamper the future growth of Fort Wayne. It wouldn't make sense for the growth of the community. It would be more a throwback to the old, rejected ideas of incorporating South Wayne, the area south of Creighton, or Waynedale, and in effect, divvying up the community.

And it probably made even less sense than those previous efforts because there wasn't any 'there' there. There was no center to West Hamilton. There was no commercial district, no identifiable downtown or center square. It wasn't Leo or Grabill or Arcola or Monroeville. There wasn't anything there. It was obviously just a ploy to stop the annexation efforts. And a pretty good ploy, too. I saw it as a serious threat that had to be dealt with.

## Helpless and exposed

The catch: There wasn't much we could do. Once the petition was filed with the commissioners, we were restricted from proposing annexation in the area unless commissioners dismissed the petition. Commissioners, meanwhile, put the entire petition under advisement for what seemed be a long time. Almost a year had gone by and they just sat on it. We were concerned; it was hard to tell how commissioners would act on it. Commissioner Ed Rousseau was against the town; Jack McComb was for it. Linda Bloom was the swing person and it wasn't clear where she stood.

All of a sudden, in the latter part of '95 and early '96, we're concerned about the future, the General Assembly and town of West Hamilton. And we hadn't even introduced anything; these were pre-emptive measures. We tried to work with commissioners and lawmakers. It finally became clear to me the tactic from the other side was to keep everything on hold, and wait for the 1997 legislative session to get through anti-annexation legislation to thwart our move in Aboite. If our hands were tied with West Hamilton and Alderman, than we were going to be in a real tricky situation.

So in 1996, we tried to figure out our strategy. We tried to work with folks. Rousseau was up for re-election that year and didn't want it to become an election issue. So part of our timing was controlled by the election schedule. We felt here's the one politician out of the three who might be the friendliest toward annexation, so no sense in making Rousseau any angrier than necessary. We tried to keep things relatively quiet until after the fall 1996 election.

## West Hamilton keeps getting larger

Meanwhile, there was an additional filing by anti-annexation folks, doubling in size the proposed town of west Hamilton. I remember walking down the first floor of the City-County Building when I saw local Pizza Hut owner Dick Freeland carrying some pizza. I love pizza. I love Pizza Hut pizza. And I said "Boy that smells great, Dick." And he was taking them up to the commissioners' office. So I either tagged along or wrangled an invitation to share some pizza. And guess what? They were meeting to talk about the West Hamilton annexation. I'm not sure they wanted me to hang around with pizza while they're doing their discussion. It became clear a lot of people were talking to the commissioners about this issue.

I was seen as the enemy. But we had an effective group here. I remember something else that really spurred me on. I got an e-mail at the end of 1996 from this young man, an IPFW student, who was active with the anti-annexation movement, Dan Lennington. And his was basically an in-your-face e-mail. It said we got you stymied because of the pending West Hamilton petition, and additional legislators were coming on board to our side. And we got great lawyers on our side. So in a sense, he was saying checkmate to us.

## The Chinese menu approach

So we waited until after the election. And we came up with a plan, sort of a Chinese menu approach. It had an option A, and an option B. I had planners work on two different annexation plans for the area. Option A was to assume West Hamilton was created and to figure out what we could annex even with it out there. Since West Hamilton could not go closer than two miles to our city limits, we could go up to the boundaries of the proposed town. Planners drew up the plan with all its inherent costs and legal obligations.

I also had them come up with option B. What would we do if West Hamilton wasn't there? We would take a larger annexation and the boundaries would be different. And we decided to have both of these plans ready to go.

### Strategy

What would we do? We argued and talked strategy. Eventually, I came up with the idea we would present both of these to City Council as option A and option B. We set it up so council would be on board with one or the other annexation plan, with whatever the council chose determined by the decision by county commissioners since they still had not acted on the West Hamilton petition. It was set up so commissioners would have to act on West Hamilton's request because it looked like they would sit on it until May 1997 when the Legislature ended its session.

If we waited, we might get stuck with some bad legislation or who knows what else. Maybe West Hamilton would have been created by this time. We just weren't confident with what commissioners might do.

The two options presented to the council, in effect, were presented to the commissioners as well. We spoke with council about this, and got its support. I preferred the option that would not have a West Hamilton. But I also feared if we had not forced the commissioners' hand we'd get stuck with all sorts of bad things.

## High noon

We determined if the commissioners rejected West Hamilton, we'd have a longer deferral date. If they didn't, we would annex the rest of the area immediately. It was something that forced the commissioners' hand. The trade-off? If you want West Hamilton, then the rest would become part of Fort Wayne almost immediately. Or get rid of West Hamilton, and annexation can wait until a later date.

Council, meanwhile, supported us. We realized the risk of the county getting angry with us. But it was a risk worth taking.

Then we met with the commissioners. They were not excited about the prospect. They didn't like their hand being forced on anything. One commissioner who we thought supported us, Ed Rousseau, didn't like it either but we believed we had few other options.

## A testy meeting

I still remember going to the commissioners' office with Payne Brown, my public safety director, and city attorney Tim McCaulay. Commissioners and county attorney Bill Fishering were there. We talked about what we were doing. My goal was to get them to buy into this concept of annexation and not get into heavy warfare with them. I wanted them to dismiss the petition.

It started out as a testy meeting. I offered our proposal, the not-so-harsh one with a deferral date. They rejected it. We went through a lot of discussion. At one stage, Rousseau came back, intentionally or not, with pretty close to what I had started out with. I told Payne and Tim ahead of time, let me run the discussion and keep your mouths' shut. I had dealt with commissioners before.

However, Payne was about ready to say Ed's proposal was similar to the one the city had originally proposed when I kicked him under the table to get him to keep his mouth shut. And we were able to get close to an agreement where the commissioners would dismiss West Hamilton's petition and we would ask council for the deferred annexation, or option B. It's what I wanted to happen.

Afterward, Payne was impressed. I told him sometimes you have to let things happen, talk them through and explain the logic, and commissioners would come around. In the end, commissioners voted 2-1 against it, with Jack McComb dissenting. Then we got council approval and assumed there would be enough signatures from Aboite residents for a court fight.

**Other battlefronts**

Meanwhile, we still had battles with legislators. And we lost at the trial court level. It was very disappointing.

I was very concerned about the timing. I made the decision in December 1998 not to run again and I had hoped we would have the Aboite annexation far enough along that my successor couldn't stop it. As of the end of 1998, we felt we were in good shape.

It would've been a lot simpler if the judge ruled against us while we were still in office because we could have filed an appeal. Since the Graham Richard administration decided to appeal, nothing was lost. But it would have saved me some worry.

Actually, when I made the decision not to run I was more concerned about a Joe Squadrito administration. I believed if he had been the new mayor, there might not have been the same decision to appeal the case. After Linda Buskirk won the primary election, I felt more confident either she or Graham Richard would appeal any court setback. I'm happy it worked out, but in retrospect, we cut the timing too close on the decision.

I still believe the city has a good opportunity to be successful on appeal. We've lost at the trial court level before on annexation issues. Hopefully, the city will pursue the matter aggressively and we'll get this thing done.

## Legacy

If Fort Wayne were to lose the Aboite annexation, what would my legacy be? Obviously, I'd be very disappointed. But I'm still proud of what we accomplished. St. Joe Township has all come in, Pine Valley is coming in, other areas as well. The city's population will increase significantly along with its tax base. The community's ability to be vital has been strengthened because of annexation, and the tough political decisions and controversies we lived through.

Aboite's in everybody's best interest. But if we can't get the whole loaf, I'm still proud of getting two-thirds. If we hadn't annexed, we'd be in a position today of declining population and tax base, and inability to deal with problems.

I'd also be disappointed because I took all those political hits and got nothing for it. It wasn't pleasant, but I had gotten used to it because of St. Joe. I'd be in the YMCA sitting in the sauna and I'd get into arguments with people on the issue. I'd argue my point; they'd argue their point. And I'd try to persuade them.

It would be tense in some social situations. I'd see people, some of them friends, disagree with me. But we remained friends.

## Personal considerations

There's so much peer pressure in neighborhoods with an issue like this. All the discussion centers around getting signatures on a petition to oppose annexation within a deadline. In Aboite, the opposition was organized from the start. And like in St. Joe, people's doors were knocked on two or three times for donations and signatures. People don't like to look their neighbor in the eye and say no, so they'd sign the petition. I'd hear from neighbors who didn't sign it and folks wouldn't understand why. I know some folks who signed the petition yet never brought up the issue of annexation with me.

After the petition against annexation was filed with the court, I got a copy of the list containing the names of all these folks. On that list, you'd see all sorts of folks who had called and asked me for favors, either as references, for awards, for help for their company, or to be involved in some civic activity. It was interesting to see how, on one hand, they could sign something that would hamper Fort Wayne's growth, while on the other, want the mayor, even as residents who didn't live in the city but still looked at me as their mayor, to promote their business or interests. I got used to it. I figured I was mayor for the entire community, not just Fort Wayne, and tried to do what's best for it.

It's hard not to personalize. However, I'm used to compartmentalizing. You remember but you do what you're supposed to do regardless. Politics, you learn, is a messy business. Going back to my first forays in politics, you figure some folks who are your friends will be against you. And you see it in other situations as well. You try not to take on a martyr complex. But I wanted to do what was right and I was willing to pay the cost for it, especially if we were going to get good results for the community.

**Comes a-haunting**

Obviously, this became an issue again politically in my 1998 U.S. Senate race against Evan Bayh. A lot of folks said there was no way I would do well, even in the GOP primary election, because of the anti-annexation fervor in Aboite Township. It's one of the most Republican and wealthy parts of the state. I believed my primary opponents thought I wouldn't even do well in my home base because of the annexation controversy.

I ended up winning an upset in the primary election.

I did better than some people thought. I carried Allen County, and folks didn't even think I would carry it. I had about 52 percent of the vote; maybe it would have been larger if I didn't have these problems.

I spoke with John Price—who did very little campaigning in Allen County—afterward and he said he was told I was so weak up here there was no way I was going to come close to getting any votes from Aboite. I believe people turned a controversial issue into an assumption I had no popularity or support at all, as people reasoned in St. Joe Township and Pine Valley.

My bottom line with Aboite: Most people don't want to be annexed and are angry at me for doing it. But they respect me as mayor and still figure me as a straight-shooter who tells it like it is. And sometimes you pay a political cost.

### Trying to talk me out of it

There was a lot of pressure. There was one meeting at GOP party chairman Steve Shine's, sometime during this whole mess. We had a lot of state legislators, party officials, county officials there and I. All I remember is the discussion got into annexation with about 20 people against it on one side and just me. Tim Berry, county treasurer at the time, may have been the only one defending me.

It was one of these get-togethers where officials discussed what was coming up in the election. They didn't want events to come unraveled. All of a sudden, they're focusing on me and annexation, and with it comes the pressure. But I told them, I have to do what I have to do. And I'm doing what I think is right. Needless to say, it doesn't go over well with people who just look at political equations.

Most of them gave up trying to change my mind on annexation. I have always been willing to talk strategy; about whether to delay it or withhold pursuing annexation during an election cycle. It was not just as a favor to them, but because I realized politicizing the issue can have some real practical drawbacks. Sometimes with issues like this, you want to keep out of politics as much as possible. Sometimes politicians talk more sensibly about issues like annexation if they don't have an election coming up in a month or two.

But it was still hard for me to understand the animosity attached to the issue and the animosity attached to the city and people who live in it. Part of it's a racial or class issue.

When I got sworn in the third time as mayor, I mentioned a line in a New York Times column about Mexico City where residents put up high walls and tinted windows to keep out those people they didn't want to be exposed to. I didn't want our community to become one of those where people believed higher walls and opaque windows would cut out what was going on. We're all in this together.

## Selfish arguments

The strident anti-annexation statements often were nothing more that a sense of, "I got mine and I don't care about you." It's an aspect that always bothers me. I get a lot of that kind of sentiment from people who live in a community where otherwise there is so much interaction. They're part of us; they're our neighbors. There's so much interconnection for people to be saying, "We don't want to pay. We don't want to be helping decide our future."

I believed such comments were very shortsighted, and from some people, very mean-spirited. It's hard to take. A lot of these people I worked with on boards and commissions, even before I became mayor. And to see that kind of approach I clearly believed was a mistake.

Part of it was the vilification. You could sense some of the hate I got in the mail and in the comments. You might disagree with me, but comparing me with Hitler, or Saddam Hussein, is getting pretty ridiculous.

## The vision thing

Does this mean the community lacks vision? It's clearly a legitimate issue. I believed I was a pretty activist mayor and not everyone agreed with the activism.

This is a town where people are used to being able to stop things. Folks opposed to annexation have been able to stop things in the past, whether it was developments they didn't like or political moves they opposed. All of sudden, I wasn't getting stopped. If the monied, powerful or other elected people couldn't stop things, there was a sense the rules were being changed as to how the community did business.

I think part of my problem with the county was the result of annexation, and it worsened my relationship with the commissioners, particularly Jack McComb. It was sort of like, "How dare you force us to make a decision." A lot of groups are used to not having to make decisions, or making them publicly or in the spotlight. But I forced the county to make a very controversial decision in the glare of the public spotlight. And it's not the way they were used to doing business.

In some sense, my single-minded push for annexation was seen as a threat to the power of others to say no to things. Part of it ties to vision. This is a community that has problems getting its act together. When it comes to a long-range vision, it's hard to get consensus on one because groups don't like giving up any of their power. It applies to elected officials or influence groups; it's one of the challenges here.

Sometimes you have to go from your position of strength, and it was seen as heavy-handed. I don't mind when people disagree with me. But I do when folks argue to keep the community in a position where it can't do things when it wants to or at least if the majority wants to or when it's clearly the right thing to do. It's a town where it's hard to do those things, like annexation, even with support because one or two groups are against it.

After 12 years, do we have vision? My view hasn't changed after being mayor. My grandfather could tell stories from the 1940s, my father from the 1960s and '70s about how groups fought over issues. I think highly of the people in this community. It's just that sometimes, it's like pulling teeth to do it.

Our greatest moments have been in response to crisis. It shows hard work and pulling together can work here. But if it's not seen as an immediate crisis, it's tough to get them on board. We fight the flood, work on economic development after International Harvester leaves, but we reject the north-south, east-west thruway in the 1940s, we don't modernize let alone consolidate local government, we fight annexation and oppose civic improvements. We've fought the airport; we've fought the baseball stadium.

One of my strengths has been that I usually can figure out ways to get people to work together or at least get enough of them to go along with a new plan. It doesn't always make people happy, but the general public has supported this issue and supported me in what I was trying to accomplish.

**Was I right?**

Was Paul Helmke right? Folks will look back and say this was something we've done to make the community strong. You won't look back at what annexation's done to taxes. Even folks in St. Joe now realize they're getting better services and taxes aren't such a burden. Recent history smoothes a lot of that over. Over 50 years, folks will wonder why was it so much of an issue.

Consider this: How could we have looked at an area south of Creighton as a separate part of town? It wouldn't have worked. Everybody knows that. How could Waynedale think about staying separate? Forty years from now this is going to be a solid, urban area. We'll be judged on how we've been able to fight crime, grow and stay vibrant. And folks will say if we hadn't been able to do these things, like annexation, we'd have our hands tied behind our backs.

There's plenty of room here to grow, at least with availability of land. Look at other communities. One of our strengths is we haven't been hemmed in by other communities, and it's why West Hamilton so concerned me.

Do we want to be like Gary surrounded by other municipalities that prevented it from growing? In most cities on the East Coast, it's the same way. Cities with elastic boundaries were ones that were able to do better in tough times and take advantage of opportunities. Older cities, the Detroits and Garys, had inelastic boundaries you couldn't shift. It's researched in such books like Cities Without Suburbs. Cities like Phoenix and Charlotte, for example, can move their boundaries. It allowed them to be stronger.

We are in a situation where we don't need to be hemmed in, and with a decent annexation law, should be able to reflect the community's growth. It should position us well in the state, in the Midwest and the country.

One of the challenges is to make sure growth doesn't get out of control. But we have the room, water and land to grow. Our biggest lack is available work force. When people realize places like this is where you can make some money, and the quality of life is good, they'll come here. But we have to make sure we've got our act together to take advantage of the opportunities that come along.

## Cast of characters:

**Greg Purcell**—Top-ranking official who served under Mayors Win Moses Jr., Paul Helmke and Graham Richard

**Bob Alderman**—State House District 83 representative for 24 years

**David Long**—State Senate District 16 representative; previously, served as 4th District City Councilman

**Jack McComb**—Allen County Commissioner who died this year; he opposed the city's annexation of Aboite

**Richard Freeland**—Aboite resident and restaurant owner

**Steve Shine**—Chairman of Allen County Republican Party; long-time local media personality

# A POLITICAL ANIMAL

When I finished my first term in 1991, I always assumed I would run for a second. It wasn't automatic, but it became clear you couldn't accomplish a lot in a four-year period.

Annexations and police changes took at least another term. I believed I was in pretty good shape. But we started to experience an economic downturn at the end of 1990, the same that affected George Bush's re-election.

The situation was tricky. I had started community-oriented policing, for example, but it took longer to accomplish. We didn't have all the success we were hoping for at the time, and crime stats were actually going up. But during neighborhood walks, I had a sense from residents I would win. So I wondered who would run against me.

In polling, we checked my numbers against Win Moses Jr., Mark GiaQuinta and Tom Henry as possible Democratic opponents. I did well against any of the well-known Democrats. By close to primary election time, it became clear those people weren't going to be running. Most of the well-known Democrats figured I'd be tough to beat.

As a result, I was surprised my opponent turned out to be Charlie Belch. I first heard about it at the YMCA, where I saw Moses. He asked did I know who was running against me. And it's when I first heard it was Charlie Belch.

## Election issues

The issues that came into play were annexation and the income-tax vote, as well as the controversy over the Adams Center Road hazardous waste landfill expansion. In the primary election, David Roach opposed me; it was the first time he had run for office.

I remember a debate with him at Indiana University-Purdue University Fort Wayne, a chance to get some publicity. We had the debate and Roach didn't know how to do it. It was something where I almost had to tell him what questions to ask me and how he were supposed to respond to what I was saying or doing. One of his campaign issues was to put a dome over the city or build a racetrack for it.

Needless to say, I won the primary. There was a 10 percent vote for Roach, the anti-Helmke vote.

## Belch and rough politics

The race against Charlie was tough. Charlie knew politics well, and understood what needed to be done. He did it well. He raised issues where I might have been weak, say on economic development.

He did a good job pulling quotes, sometimes out of context, from newspaper clipping about when different businesses were doing cutbacks or leaving town. He arranged them as a list of failures: "When Falstaff left, Helmke said that's not my job. When November, comes along, it's time to tell Helmke, it's not your job."

It was a pretty effective piece of speechifying and campaign literature. It's tough being mayor; you're blamed for things out of your control. On economic development, the beer business is beyond your control, although I think I quipped we weren't drinking enough beer.

He tried to score points on the crime issue as well. A print piece of his went a bit too far. It raised the issue of crime, saying look at Chicago, Detroit and then, Fort Wayne. We're in a crime wave. Blame Helmke for it.

He made a good argument politically but it didn't resonate with the public. People saw what we were doing to curb crime and attract jobs.

## Belch and taxes

I was attacked on COIT. I wasn't so concerned about defending the income tax, because it was a part of our fiscal recovery package. But there was talk Charlie was going to say that I had said I wasn't going to raise taxes, and of course, it was something Bush was getting attacked for. We had to do our own research to counter the argument; I found one clip where I said I wasn't going to raise taxes until I had a chance to see the books and study the city's financial situation. Then we had to pre-empt the media on the tax issue. I was willing to fight Charlie on the tax issue, but I didn't want folks to believe I had broken a promise.

We put together an ad campaign, and brought in a political media consultant. We talked in commercials about our accomplishments.

One of our concerns was that Charlie could go negative on us. We tried to pre-empt Charlie with an ad, attempted in a humorous sort of way. We tried to publicize the fact of Charlie's background as a political organization person. He was the 4th District Democrat chairman.

As a result, we put together an ad called "Smoke-filled Rooms" where you saw people playing poker, and all you saw were their hands. It talked about Belch's background as a backroom-type of politician. We pulled out some quote where he said good things about Mayor Richard Daley's machine system in Chicago. We had a picture of Win Moses Jr., and he was with Daley.

We tried to point out to voters that whatever they had heard from Charlie, to remember it was being said by a rough-and-tumble political figure. And Charlie was good in that role.

## Debates

We had several debates. Our argument was, he just didn't get it. The issues he was bringing up, we had already taken steps to correct. But he was a tough opponent, and he was a gentleman, too. I liked him and got along with him.

I wound up winning with about 59 percent, a very solid win.

The one thing I wasn't sure of was how the first phases of the St. Joseph Township annexation would affect the election. I remember saying, "What a lousy time to bring in these disgruntled voters into the city just two months before the election."

We still won nearly all those areas, although the numbers could have been less than the typical GOP results in the suburbs. We also picked up another Republican on council; it became 6-3 Democrat. It showed that despite some people who said the only reason I won in 1987 was as because of an anti-Moses vote, the 1991 vote showed people supported what I was trying to do for the community. I was very encouraged by the 59 percent win; it was a good stamp of approval.

## Staying put

Meanwhile, I had looked closely at running for Dan Coats' congressional seat in 1989 when he gave it up to become U.S. senator. I felt I could have won. I had good approval ratings as mayor, but I was in the middle of too many things—COIT and annexation, for example—and it wouldn't be good timing.

Those were two issues I was committed to. By running, I'd be sacrificing the income tax and annexation for my own political agenda. I also believed people didn't like politicians who just jump from office to office. I had been mayor just a year, and that would have been jumping off too quickly. I was voted in for a four-year job and I felt I needed to live up to the voters' choice of me as mayor.

Some people thought I'd more enjoy being a legislator. But I enjoyed being mayor. I enjoyed being in charge and I wasn't sure I'd like to be in Congress, in a minority party as well.

## For Congress

So I decided not to run; there was a lot of maneuvering by others for the job. Prosecutor Steve Sims was making noise about it; Dan Heath, my campaign manager, was interested in it. Also state legislator Mitch Harper and Jeff Turner, who was part of Coats' inner circle, were interested. I decided to back Dan Heath. I backed him big, and got involved in the campaign to get him elected in the GOP caucus. It was one of the most exciting political events of a long time.

It was a caucus that went several rounds among the GOP precinct committee members. Sims had dropped at this stage. Sims apparently felt he had been promised a lot more support than he had gotten. Les Gerig, the longtime CEO of Mutual Security Life, was on board for him and Sims believed it would deliver a lot of Coats support since Gerig had been a longtime Coats mentor.

There was some rumbling Gerig had switched his support to Jeff Turner or withdrawn his support. It was interesting that Sims' deputy, and at one time my public safety director, Michael McAlexander, was jockeying to become prosecutor. And he had it lined up with then-Gov. Robert Orr to get named prosecutor while Orr was still governor. So there was a timetable for Sims to make his decision.

It's amazing, once you leave office, how much jockeying goes on.

## Heath wins

Heath ends up winning, even though you got a lot of the old Coats' people backing Jeff Turner. It came down to Turner and Heath. Harper's people eventually went to Heath more than Turner. I felt good about it. It showed I had good political clout within the party for my support of Heath.

Then things turned for the worse. National Republicans came in to help. Heath ran against Jill Long, who had lost twice before. She was a good candidate, and attacked Heath for the things the city was doing, like annexation and income tax. It tied into the anti-annexation feelings.

The timing was about the worst possible; the election was at a time of anti-annexation animosity. Long used those to her advantage. Meanwhile, the national Republicans told Heath not to associate himself with me, to pretend not to know me.

Barbara Bush came to town, and I was asked specifically not to show up at the airport or at the campaign event at a local high school. This was the first lady of the United States and it didn't make much sense. But I wasn't the political expert. I believed they were wrong, but I wanted Heath to win, so I stayed out. And I didn't go.

My advice would have been to address the issues, and argue the actions were needed because of the lousy shape Moses had left city finances in. A simple explanation could have been, "Blame Moses for the problems." Instead of taking that kind of simplistic political response, their way was to question who's Helmke and that these issues weren't relevant to Congress.

## Heath loses

These concerns were never really met head-on. Long won for 4th District Congress in a close race.

I still blame the national Republicans for screwing up the race. Long, meanwhile, turned out to be good for Fort Wayne. She worked closely with us for flood control funding, for example.

While I blamed her campaign for tarnishing my image and making it a bit tougher to live down that negative reputation on taxes and annexation, those issues weren't responded to by Heath. Maybe I should have responded on my own to those charges, but I didn't want to mess up Heath's election. All the attacks came without an answer, which experts in politics say is the worst kind of situation. And I've spent a lot of the last 10 years responding to the charges Jill Long first brought up.

I didn't consider running in any of the elections against Jill Long once she got into office. But by 1994, she was perceived as vulnerable, and Mark Souder defeated her. By then, I really enjoyed being mayor and didn't really give running for Congress a lot of thought.

By 1994, I had already gotten some flak for supporting the Clinton stimulus package a year earlier. By the time of the GOP primary election that Souder won for the right to challenge Long, I didn't see Congress necessarily as a step up from being mayor. I enjoyed being mayor and enjoyed being in charge.

**Did I blow it?**

If the goal was to get to Washington, then I blew it by not running when situations presented themselves. I felt pretty confident I could have gone to Washington in 1989 if I had wanted to. Even though folks don't like you jumping office, I was well-known with a good approval rating and could have won easily, especially since Heath, with no name recognition, came within a point of winning the race.

Instead, I became more active in national issues through the National League of Cities and U.S. Conference of Mayors.

## A third term

Meanwhile, I decided to run for a rare third term as mayor. It was a tougher decision, however, to run a third time in 1995. By then, we had made a lot of progress. Community-oriented government was just taking root.

I remember speaking to neighborhood groups about community-oriented policing and community-oriented government. Some people said it sounds good, but success depended a lot on Police Chief Neil Moore and me bringing this along. "How do we know you're going to be there with the election just a year away? We don't want to invest a lot of time and effort in this new way of doing things if someone new is going to shoot it down," they argued.

I took the opinion to heart. It was a new philosophy for local government and the Police Department. I became convinced those initiatives weren't far enough along they would be there in the future.

My challenge was more with rumblings in the local party, with talk that Sheriff Joe Squadrito was going to take me on in the primary election. This was when GOP Chairman Steve Shine orchestrated a meeting with Squadrito, himself and me at the Fort Wayne Country Club in late 1994 to make peace, and to prevent attacks from the sheriff on me. This was at a time Squadrito was second-guessing a lot of things we were doing in the Police Department.

We had put together a plan to work closely with Metro Squad, a joint police effort with the city and county. There were tensions with him, but I still tried.

So here we're in this private room, just the three of us, with some discussions about politics and police. We wound up smoking cigars and drinking cognac. As a result, Squadrito decided not to run.

I had a few primary election opponents this time. One was a city utility worker; the other, a janitor. Still, it was good to get publicity. I won big time as expected, and saw only scant party dissatisfaction.

## Vs. Essex and Kempf

I ran against Tom Essex, who was Wayne Township Trustee. He was a candidate to take seriously, and a person who had worked for the city when I had started, as a labor relations official.

He always treated me well, and had even given me a book once for my birthday.

The race also had a Libertarian, Bill Kempf, which made it interesting. He was someone who believed the federal income tax was unconstitutional and people shouldn't be paying it.

Most of the campaign was a referendum on what I had done. The economy was in good shape; unemployment was down, although crime was still serious. We were making progress with money for new police officers from the federal Crime Bill. We ran ads talking about what we had done, and won re-election with close to 65 percent of the vote.

Republicans captured a majority, 5-4 on council; the first time since around 1967. I felt good and we were in solid shape.

## Looking around

After the third election in 1995, I'm pretty sure I'm not going to run again. I started to look around although nothing was happening. I assumed the Senate race in 1998 would be Evan Bayh vs. Dan Coats. As a result, it was a shock politically to me when the incumbent, Coats, announced in late 1996 he wasn't going to run again.

With an open seat, you look at it seriously. An open primary was probably my best shot to get a statewide nod. At this stage, however, I'm hearing otherwise: "You're too liberal. You're a friend of Clinton. You've raised taxes. You're too moderate. You're not Republican enough."

People also didn't want to risk nominating me for lieutenant governor; there was this feeling I'd never get a slot in a GOP convention.

## Vs. Rusthoven and Price

As a result, my best possibility was an open statewide primary. Peter Rusthoven and John Price jump into the race. As I watch what's developing, I realize I can win this primary election. It was obvious to me beating Bayh was going to be tough, but establishing myself with the statewide Republican Party that I was someone to be looked at seriously was important to me.

In July 1997 I decided to run, believing I could win because I had good name recognition in this part of the state and was the only one of the three who had won an election. Most of the organized party was behind Rusthoven; he had most of the county chairmen, and the moneyed people. Even in Allen County, he had Sheriff Joe Squadrito, Pizza Hut magnate Dick Freeland and State Sen. David Long behind him.

But I believed I was stronger than some people were giving me credit for. I wanted to check out what it would take to run statewide. I put together a campaign on a shoestring.

## My Republican credentials

My early battle was establishing my Republican credentials and winning the primary. There were several Lincoln Day dinners in various counties, and many of them had all three of us on the agenda. Eventually, you start learning your opponents' speeches by heart. I enjoyed it.

A big challenge was trying to collect petitions to get on the ballot. To get on the ballot for senator or governor, you need 500 signatures from registered voters on a petition, 500 from each congressional district. It doesn't sound like a lot, just 5,000 signatures altogether. But most people are reluctant to sign anything, and the place you get these signatures is at these Lincoln Day dinners.

I was starting a lot later than the others and was behind by the start of 1998; it had to be done by mid-February. We're playing catch-up, and the dinners are the easiest way to do it. Standing at a shopping mall, for example, you might get signatures from people who aren't registered voters or don't live in the district. It's a screwy system, and we weren't sure we were going to get it.

The hardest area was around Indianapolis: two congressional districts there, the 10th and 6th. It's hard to figure out where the boundary lines are. So when we went to political events in Indianapolis, we weren't sure if folks were signing for the 10th or the 6th. You can't put two different districts on the same sheet of paper because you can only send it to one clerk. So a petition with two sets of names gets counted as only one set from one district. You can't send the other set of signatures from that same petition to another clerk.

We got real worried about the 10th District, where there's more Democrats. We had misspellings, bad addresses; those would get thrown out.

It's the final day in mid-February. I'm heading to Evansville after a speech. My campaign manager, Peter Slen, picked me up and we're trying to get information on the phone about how we're doing with signatures in each of the 10 districts. The one my manager is waiting on is the 10th District. We finally get the call around 5:30 p.m. and we're about 30 people more than we need.

My campaign manager stops the van and goes out to throw up because of nerves. If we had come up with 490, for example, we wouldn't be on the ballot. If we hadn't gotten the right number of signatures, I was going to suggest pulling over at a bar on the way to Evansville and drinking away our sorrows instead of continuing the trip.

## In the primary

During the primary, we were in southern Indiana for a debate with the other two. One question was on gun control. I was a firm supporter of the Brady Bill and the assault weapon ban. I support common sense gun measures.

I led off by telling southern Indiana Republicans I'm a firm believer in the Second Amendment, but you can have common sense gun measures because I'd seen the results of shootings in the streets of Fort Wayne. It didn't go over well with the crowd.

Meanwhile, Rusthoven's view was there was no need for more legislation. Price's view was that every person ought to have a gun and carry it. The crowd is getting all revved up and my campaign manager is in the back gesturing: If we had to beat a hasty retreat, this was the way to the exit.

But people respected my views even if they were things people didn't want to hear. Polls showed it a close race; experts predicted I'd come in third. The Indiana Policy in Review, other publications, none had me winning.

## I win

I knew it would be a close, uphill race. On Election Day in May, the returns were so slow. All of us are in the 30 percent range. Finally, with more than 80 percent tallied, I pull ahead with a 1 or 2 percent lead. But Allen County had not yet turned in all its results. While I expected to do well there and expected Allen County would boost my lead at the time, who knew? With folks in Aboite Township upset with me over annexation, with the Squadrito, Freeland, Long group maybe delivering the county to another candidate, who knew?

Finally, around midnight I realize I had won. I ended up winning 35 percent; the others got 33 and 32 percent.

**So now what?**

I won the U.S. Senate primary, and I'm excited. Then the issue is how to put together a decent campaign against Bayh, and I recognize it's going to be an uphill race.

At this stage, I'm looking toward the party for support. One of the biggest disappointments was how little structural support I got from the party. I'm looking primarily at the state party. I'm getting a lot of good moral support but basically, no money and no real organization. We got some space in the state Republican headquarters and we might have been charged even for that.

I had hoped there would have been more guidance, structure and money and help we could have had from the state party.

I'm not naive about politics, but I believed the party itself was stronger than it actually was. Over the years, political parties aren't as strong as they used to be. The state party has lost a lot of clout; it lost the 1996 gubernatorial race when it had a lot of money and a very attractive candidate in Steve Goldsmith.

Legislative control was pretty even, but Democrats had a lot of say. The party had a lot of trouble raising money, in part because it didn't have control of the governor's office. For a lot of the party officials, the situation was like this: "Things are tight, the senatorial race is an uphill battle. Let's put the focus on getting enough seats in the Legislature to get control there." I can understand the outlook but I still had hoped there would have been more help.

## Thanks for nothing

Another big disappointment was the lack of help I got from the national Republican Party. They were considering the race a long shot, but as the campaign developed, there was nothing from the national party. I felt there should have been something.

For me, the real kick in the teeth came near the end, when we were on television with debates and are looking for more dollars to get more television time than we had been able to afford. The national Republicans sent out a letter saying how it was important to hold Dan Coats' seat and how important it was to send the national Republican Party money.

When I heard about the letter, I called them up and said, "You are using my race as a way to get money. You're sending this letter to potential contributors in Indiana. Am I going to be able to see any money from this?" They said no. To me, it smacked of false advertising. Send your dollars today but we're not going to use it to try to hold on to Dan Coats' seat.

## Misguided strategy

The other frustration with national Republicans concerned where they were putting money. I pointed out to them they were putting money into the California Senate race; from what I had read, the GOP was in an uphill battle there, too. They ended up losing the race.

I tried to let them know a dollar goes a lot farther in Indiana than California, just a couple of hundred thousand, anything. Fifty thousand, $100,000 buys a lot of TV time in Indiana. It didn't move them one bit. It was a cold-hearted analysis my race wasn't on their radar screen. They had written it off from the start. I know, if Coats was the candidate, they would have paid more attention. Instead, they put their money elsewhere.

It's the name of the game with federal elections. If it looks like you are behind from the start, the national party isn't going to do anything to make it closer. I believed I had credibility as a candidate, was a successful mayor for many years, was president of the U.S. Conference of Mayors. Yet the political analysts described me as the best candidate who was going to get wiped out in the fall.

We ended up raising $700,000; Bayh raised about $7 million. With that kind of disparity, the race is almost over before it starts. With our limited resources, we weren't able to do television advertising in Fort Wayne. But Bayh was running heavy ads here attacking me, and I couldn't respond.

### A tough lesson

What did I learn from all this? It's going to be a long time before I send a check to the national Republican Party. I'll send it to my candidate of choice from now on.

The situation certainly didn't make me get any closer to the national party structure. Even a token amount of support would have helped. The GOP usually raises a heck of a lot of money. If the party isn't going to help those people who've helped the party in the past, than there will be less loyalty to it. It's clearly my reaction personally and from a lot of people who supported me and had sent checks to the national party. When they realized what the party was doing, their attitude was they were going to stop sending checks to the party as well.

### Frustrations

The frustration with the campaign was to engage Bayh. In the primary election, at least there always was an event where opponents and I showed up. It lent itself to a lot of discussion. Against Bayh, there was less of it. There were just a few debates, a few news conferences. From Bayh's perspective, of course, he didn't want to get engaged. But for me, and a voter who's trying to make a decision, it didn't help.

Debate serves the voter, and the system, well. It was difficult to handle with Bayh, because he tried to delay the engagement as long as possible. What's smart for politics often isn't good for the system.

We tried to push Bayh to debate, and we did a few at the end. It was tricky with Bayh: Whenever I'd raised an issue, he'd agreed with me. We tried to come up with issues that would show a difference between us. Instead, so often he agreed with me on issues. His response was that he agreed with me.

Obviously, his campaign was based on trying to make him look as much a Republican as possible, or at least a centrist Republican. It made it difficult to engage him on issues because of the strategy. What were the lines of difference? Whenever I brought up something, he'd agree with me. He wasn't coming up with ideas on his own.

Bayh was always polite; you never really felt angry with him. The tough part was trying to find out what was there; what was he thinking about? It was almost so neat, so well-scripted, so well-groomed. I kept waiting to find out if he was a robot, like one of the old "Twilight Zone" episodes where you cut the skin and there's wire underneath.

**Bayh and self-control**

It showed, however, how good Evan was at self-control and keeping emotions in check. The only time I saw him get riled up was back in 1990, when I did a fly-around for Bill Hudnut when he was running for secretary of state. Bayh was governor, and his man Joe Hogsett was running against Hudnut for secretary of state. I was stumping for Hudnut.

A few days later, I'm in Indy, and had to be in Fort Wayne as well that day. It got so I was going to fly back to Fort Wayne with the governor. So I get out to the airport and Bayh is very cold to me. As he starts walking toward the plane, Bayh looks over his shoulder to the back where I'm following, and he says he didn't like the nasty things I was saying about him or Susan during my fly-around with Hudnut.

I thought, "Where's my car?" But my people had already left; I didn't know how it would be to fly back with that guy.

We got to the plane, and it was one of the few times I saw him show any real emotion. He's somebody who can show emotion, but he's very controlled, and stayed that way throughout the Senate campaign.

**Engaging the enemy**

One time, however, we're trying to engage him with a television ad. It showed what I had done in Fort Wayne, with a clip of Bayh introducing Clinton at a rally in Michigan City in 1996. Obviously, this is during the Clinton impeachment, and Republicans had been pushing me to tie Bayh with Clinton. The ad then showed Bayh speaking, and afterward, he used the word values. And we used the tag line of "values." We were criticized for dirty politics; Democrats came down hard on us for it.

Another time, Susan Bayh had been named to some Great Lakes, U.S. and Canada commission, a sort of cushy job. It deals with trade and boundary issues, although we laughed that the commission's job was to make sure we didn't go to war with Canada, and so far, it's been successful. She's on this commission, and got paid about $80,000 a year. In one of our debates, I brought it up in the context of how could Bayh judge Clinton fairly if his family is getting $80,000 from a Clinton appointment?

At the debate, Susan was sitting in the front row, next to my brother, Mark. She was very upset by my mention of her. Bayh didn't say anything to me, but he was bristling some. It really didn't rattle him at the debate, but his campaign manager came up to me afterward and said, "How dare you do that?" Bayh's used to having things run smoothly for him.

## The best politician?

I still believe Win Moses is one of the best at politics. In a lot of ways, Moses was tougher to go against in debates than Bayh. Bayh was structured, and had a "don't make mistakes" kind of approach to things. With Moses, you were never sure what he was going to do. Win's bright and he's able to shift gears or throw something unexpected at you. With Bayh, it would rarely be unexpected.

On election night, the numbers came in solidly against me, like the polls had said. Final numbers showed I was beaten by about 28 percentage points.

## The road show

I always got treated pretty well in other parts of the state. It's just that my name ID outside Fort Wayne was pretty low. There were some party chairmen and activists who were supportive, but it's tough to get your name out if it's the first time you are running statewide.

One of the fun things we did was a weeklong bus tour of the state. It started in Fort Wayne, and had a lot of stops. By the end of the trip, the bus was getting trashy and smelly, and you wound up passing places because you weren't sure where it was.

We were in eastern Indiana to see Jean Ann Harcourt, who had been a national committee person, and was a neat woman. She has a factory where they make pencils and school supplies. It's a small town off the beaten path. We had to take an unmarked side road through the middle of a cornfield, and it's as high as the window. We had to drive the bus nearly off the road whenever a car came from the other direction. It was like being in some horror movie, the Land of the Corn.

You'd get these lonely moments on the road, but they were balanced out with good times. I really enjoyed campaigning. I liked seeing new places and meeting new people. While Indiana has different concerns and issues, it contains good-hearted people.

## A better politician

I've become a better politician over the years. Many people who've seen me say I'm a lot more relaxed. A lot of politics is self-confidence. You feel you can answer any questions and handle any issues. And you do better if you're not uptight.

Experience helps a lot. Giving speeches constantly as mayor, you get better. I did a good job with the Senate race because of my background and knowledge of national issues. I've improved a lot with my people skills. I used to be a lot more shy than I am now, but I've gotten a lot better working a crowd and going table to table.

It's a lot easier in Fort Wayne, when you're well-known, to walk through a diner and shake hands with customers. What I'm weak at as a politician, however, is attack. I can attack if attacked first. But I try not to get nasty. Sometimes in politics, folks want you to do the "red meat, chew them up and get nasty" way of politicking. Supporters would have liked to have seen more of it against Bayh. But I wasn't going to get nasty; it's not my style.

## Looking at myself in the mirror

I want to be able to look myself in the mirror, say I raised good issues, but in a fair way. Maybe it limits me as a politician, but on one level, it's what most people want from a politician.

You have to stay civil; these are people you are going to continue dealing with. If you disagree, do it fairly and aboveboard.

I tend to confuse my opponents because I'm not your normal politician. In the Senate primary, I was considered not a serious threat because my opponents didn't perceive me as a "real Republican." They didn't think I'd appeal to people and wouldn't get treated seriously.

There also was the perception I was too controversial and independent. Party types like folks who follow the party line. defined the party line, instead of what someone told me the party line is. I tried to define Republicanism my way. As a result, they considered me a weak primary election candidate.

Against Bayh, there was a sense I wasn't going to be real nasty and could be dealt with differently. I wasn't going to be a bomb thrower coming out of nowhere.

### Helmke, the leftist

Often, Democratic pundits tried to position me to the left and Bayh to the center. That way, Democrats wouldn't vote for me and Evan would take over the great center. They tried to give Bayh the conservative label and to marginalize me on the left.

They attacked me for having raised taxes. It really bothered me when you look at things logically, although you should never do that in politics. Bayh's position was that economic development should be carried out on the local level. But when I did that, the response was, "Oh, he raised taxes a few times!"

### Waiting for a tidal wave

Bayh's people were more concerned how the Clinton mess was going to affect them. So they tried to stay away from Clinton, and the Democrat label, and paint me as more liberal than they.

The only real shot I had to win was if there was a serious tidal wave against Clinton that turned against Democrats, but it didn't happen. I was hoping for a tidal wave and instead, I got one going the other way on me that helped Democrats.

**No one to talk to**

I learned the mayor's job doesn't offer too many people who you can talk to about broad issues. Talking with other mayors facing similar problems was one of the best ways to bounce off issues on how to deal with crime and drugs. Maybe you're competing with their cities, but such feedback gave you insight on how to do things differently.

Having someone from Akron come here and look at our city, and tell us their impressions, was good. We put out a lot of promotional stuff, so did other cities; but it was good to have someone look at the other side of what we were doing. It was a way to promote our city. I believed if I could be with a national organization like the U.S. Conference of Mayors, and be seen on CNN or quoted in Time magazine as mayor of Fort Wayne, I was helping promote the city. It got the name out there; it's good advertising.

**Stay home, young man**

I'm used to the criticism that this kind of approach was my way of hogging the limelight. It's shortsighted. There were folks who criticized me any time I left the city. It's ridiculous to think that I could do this job just by sitting inside the city limits.

You've got to go out and learn from others, to promote yourself and lobby for federal dollars. We were trying to get money for the airport, the flood control project and for transportation improvements.

I had gone out with the Airport Authority at one time to make a presentation on airport issues and needs. Later, I had a meeting with the Conference of Mayors, and I told local airport officials I was sure I could meet with the transportation secretary. I met with the secretary, told him I had met him before and these were the local issues of concern. I passed along my card and sent him information, and in a few weeks, we got approval.

Being able to do some personal lobbying of the Cabinet is very important. People pay a lot of money to get lobbyists just inside the door to speak with these people. I'm standing around and speaking with them on a regular basis, and not just because I'm a mayor, but as president of the Conference of Mayors. It got us some inside contact, and it translated into dollars.

It paid off for the city. But then I'd see these letters to the editor, "He shouldn't leave the city until he's fixed every sewer and pothole." Yet, you were were able to do these things because you were getting the federal dollars or stopping federal mandates. The most ridiculous one involved a piece by the Indiana Policy Review about me, a cover story. They talked about how much time I had traveled out of the city. One time I was giving a speech in Pine Valley, and they counted it as going outside the city.

Excuse me. Why can't I attend a meeting or an organization that meets in Allen County but outside the city limits without being accused of excessive traveling outside the city? The argument showed they're crazy.

The presidency of the conference of mayors was a real honor, a one-year term as top dog of all mayors from cities over 30,000 in population. We never had a Fort Wayne mayor hold the position. Lugar and Hudnut, both of Indianapolis, had been president of the National League of Cities, the other organization, and it's prestigious as well. Richard Hatcher of Gary was the only other Indiana president of the Conference of Mayors.

It put Fort Wayne more on the map. I enjoyed it. Despite the time it took, I kept things in balance.

**Sister Cities**

Sister Cities, meanwhile, is a program we've been involved with since about 1976 and it started with the first city, Takaoka, Japan. It created a lot of opportunities by helping us contact Japanese businesses looking at the Fort Wayne area.

We had one meeting with an older Japanese gentleman, a head of a company, with the aid of a translator. One of his concerns was how will his company be treated? Any anti-Japanese backlash? He was concerned about it. But the fact we had a Sister City with Takaoka, where he wasn't from, put those fears to rest. This is a city with a strong relationship with a Japanese community that shows we weren't going to hold their Japanese nationality against them.

A lot of our Sister City programs provided cultural acclimation for school-children; it showed them how we are competing worldwide. Every year, five Japanese students would come here or five from Fort Wayne would travel overseas.

We also developed ties in Poland with Plock. Why would you do Poland? You learn; this was an Eastern European country where we got a chance to open things up. We did the same with Gera, Germany, especially with our German heritage here. It's been a good one as well.

It's not just getting jobs or businesses to invest here. It's also being part of a way to avoid getting into wars with other countries if you treat them like your sister.

**What's next?**

Where do I stand now with politics? The Senate race was exhausting, but I enjoyed it and would do it again. It was fun except for the last night. I didn't have the enthusiasm to take on another mayoral term right away, and the reality of even another campaign.

But I remain interested in politics and government. That stage of my career isn't necessarily over and done with. I want to remain involved in public policy. Whether I run for public office again, I don't know. If the right opportunity comes along, I will. If it doesn't, there's other ways to get involved.

You never know for sure; you wait to see what happens. I'm still fascinated by the issue of how people govern themselves. That's what it's all about. How do you excite them, how do you balance competing interests? I have a lot I can add to an organization, and I can do a good job as an elected or appointed official, or even in consulting. Whether it's as a lawyer giving advice to mayors and governmental officials, or in academia dealing with public policy, I want to stay involved. I like dealing with public policy and politicians. Politicians do think a little bit differently. I can speak their language.

The challenge is how do we make government work for us, with changing technology, like the Internet. How do you set up government that will have people's confidence? Those are the challenges.

**Fort Wayne's home**

Fort Wayne's home, even if I'm working somewhere else. I'll have ties here, even if I don't have a home here. Fort Wayne defines me; you need to have a base in politics. It's where my heart is. It's a good community, where my family's been involved and part of. I don't want to give that up, but I'd like to take those lessons from here and maybe apply them elsewhere.

We're 200,000 people; Fort Wayne's a decent size. We have an independent identity. As mayor, I had an opportunity to make a difference. I can drive around town and say that park is there because I pushed to get it there. You play a role in almost everything that goes on in town.

There are others who play a role with you, but the power of mayor also can keep things from getting stopped, whether it meant Headwaters Park, Courtyard Green or the baseball stadium. When you're making those decisions and they involve risk and political capital, they're not always easy decisions. You're spending dollars and staff time, and making some people with different perspectives angry. But you push them through. When you drive around and see the things you had a hand in happening, it's a good feeling. It doesn't matter if your name is on a plaque or not, it's a feeling you made the community a better place.

It's the same when at the grocery store. Folks know who you are. Sometimes they complain, and now that I'm out, it seems more people compliment than complain. Maybe because now when I get complaints, I say, "Call the other guy!" Folks have always been nice. Even when they complain, they are usually decent. At some level, government is easy.

**A happening job**

The trickiest thing is you're dealing with so many different issues. The mayor's job isn't very structured; you're jumping from police issues, to economic development issues, to park issues. You have a little bit of everything constantly.

Even if you tried to focus on one thing as top priority, events would make you shift out of necessity. You had to become a little bit of an expert in everything but with experts around you to get things done. It made it challenging. It was fun coming in just about every day because you didn't know what was going to happen. You never had one day quite like the other. It could be the weird phone call or an unforeseen incident that made you shift gears.

Life right now is a little calmer; it's off the hectic treadmill. But part of the excitement was not knowing what would come up. That living-on-the-edge kind of feeling, I did a good job of handling. I don't like to be bored and you are never bored with the mayor's job.

I probably could have stayed on and coasted; I know some mayors who are probably doing that right now. One of my strengths, however, was I always brought a lot of enthusiasm to the job. If I stayed another term, I don't know if I would have had the same enthusiasm and whether I would wind up overstaying my welcome. I sort of felt I might have enough for the rest of 1999 and even this year, but not for the rest of the term. It would have been unfair to the people and to me as well.

Sometimes, shaking things up is good.

I didn't want to get to the stage where people were opposing initiatives because I was the one proposing them. My controversial stands on some issues, like annexation, could have led to that kind of result on similar issues in the future. It wasn't happening, but it was getting to the stage where I wanted to make sure proposals weren't being rejected just because they came from me.

## Unigov

The most frustrating thing was not being able to do more with the structure of government. I always tried to get people to think about things outside the box, to look at things differently as if things weren't always this way. I used to carry around a map, and ask people to envision that they had come from another planet and had to decide how to operate government. How would they set it up, the delivery of police and fire services being just two examples? There isn't anyone who would set it up as we have.

You wouldn't draw up these boundary lines, you probably wouldn't have townships, and you'd do a lot of things differently. So, I'd tell them to look at it like there was no past and create something new. I couldn't get people to do it. Instead, people would say that's how things have always been and how they should be. Even if not, it's too hard to change. I tried to point out what we have now was brand-new in 1850, some of what we did then, like townships, made sense then because they dealt with services you needed daily. You needed townships of such a small size where you could walk to the township schools, hear the fire alarm and help your neighbor rebuild your barn. They were things you could walk to.

And counties made sense. They were things you could ride your horse to in one day. Or twice a month you needed to go to the county seat.

Today, that governmental structure doesn't reflect the fact we have the telephone and car, much less the Internet and television. We need to look at these things anew. A lot of how we structured government was based on how quickly we could interact with others.

Townships, as a result, are irrelevant today. Counties, maybe, could do the things the townships used to do and we could do away with townships. An urban county, it makes more sense to have a city government structure, where a strong executive and a city council run the show.

County structure is set up to deal with rural issues, where in the past the commissioners met once a month. It's why there are three of them. They also were the legislative body and got together only once a month. Maybe we ought to be looking at a multi-county area. The congressional district here plays the role the county used to play. Most of northeast Indiana looks at Fort Wayne as the capital. This is where the news comes from.

This is where people come to shop and for entertainment. We now work with Auburn and Huntington on transportation and economic development plans. We used to be uncooperative because they were the competition. They're not the competition anymore. Even if a business isn't locating here but in Whitley County, it's not a loss for us. Those people, because of our importance as a center, are still spending their money and time in Fort Wayne.

**Resistance**

Our old township and county lines have been outmoded to a great extent. I've had a lot of ideas how this all could be set up. It didn't have to be one way. But I wanted people to think about redrawing the structure to make it fit with what has happened over the past 150 years.

But there was so much resistance to it. We got Sen. Tom Wyss, R-Fort Wayne, to introduce a charter county government bill. We pushed for more local control, and some charter authority for here from the Legislature, which otherwise calls the shots in these areas. But the concept never went too far.

We tried to use a Consensus Committee to get folks to think about new ideas. It sort of fell over on its weight. It was the suspicion of let's not let the politicians get involved too much. The lesson I learned is you need a group with the authority to get things done. It's what I believe happened with the Consensus Committee. We had boycotts from some elected officials, and attempts to frustrate from other elected officials. As a result, the effort became reports on a shelf instead of ideas put to action.

Here, we were trying to paint the big picture and folks were saying, "Let's combine the parks departments." It makes sense to combine them, but you don't want to use all your political capital on that and skip combining the executive branches of city and county government. If we advocated incremental change, people argued against it because of the slippery slope argument. If you went with a large change, people said you were going too big too quickly. So we wound up going nowhere on these issues.

Before I was mayor, I tried to push for these changes with such groups as Fort Wayne Future, whose members worked on a vision for the community. One of the lessons I learned is you can't do it without someone on the inside, like the mayor or some other elected official. When I got elected, I started to do it. Then I was looked at too suspiciously. "Helmke's power hungry. It's a power grab."

I knew what I was doing. I worked as an assistant county attorney for 14 years. I knew their system and setup. When I was on the inside, I couldn't find any outside support. And you needed support of the Greater Fort Wayne Chamber of Commerce, the business community and neighborhoods, in addition to from politicians.

I had to make skeptics realize they were getting messed over when the system wasn't being changed to reflect changing times. Here, we're paying a ditch assessment to the county surveyor, a storm-water fee to the city, and yet our back yards are still flooded.

## Myopic

The business community saw the issue in terms of taxes. Should we have an income tax? How do we handle zoning and permit issues? No one group is in charge of the tax rate. The same was true with zoning and permits for businesses. And that makes it tough to do business here.

To me, it never mattered what you called the new system. I was even open to the idea of getting rid of the city and its boundary lines, and having everybody in the county vote for an executive responsible for the entire county.

Taxes would be paid for the entire county law enforcement, as well as planning and highway departments. It meant county commissioners would be in charge. But the county tax rate would go up to handle these urban areas in Fort Wayne as well.

At the same time, people would question whether the Fort Wayne area needed three people as executives to run local government. Hopefully, there would have been a move to have just one commissioner. Then you'd have what I've advocated all along: one executive.

Regardless if you do away with city government or county government, we need to have a jurisdictional area that makes sense, and right now it doesn't.

Even if it was done on a countywide basis, like Indianapolis, it would make more sense to call the new setup Fort Wayne, not Allen County. It's like dealing in product brands. There's higher product identification with Fort Wayne than Allen County.

It didn't have to be me as mayor; it didn't have to be the city in charge. We could have gotten rid of elected county officials only after several years had gone by, until everyone finished their elected terms.

### Hard to get a quick response

On big issues, the city and county worked together. The divisions, however, were noticed in the little details. When somebody needed something, like in economic development, you couldn't just say yes but you had to wait until the city and county got together for a response. Maybe it resulted in a delay of an hour or a delay of a day, but it risked that a prospective business would wind up going elsewhere.

We would try to resolve issues regarding lot size requirements, for example. For new developments, we worked with the county not to make the requirements that much different than the city's urban standards if those new areas were just a few years from being annexed into Fort Wayne. Sometimes we got things worked out; other times, not.

Almost every day, an issue came up where it would have been a lot easier if some one person was in charge, not several. It wasn't like I was always right. Instead, we don't have a mechanism to resolve disputes in the community. You could have hard-fought battles with the City Council and mayor, but there's a process where the issue comes to a head and you vote.

But when it's an issue of city vs. county, there's no way to resolve it. Maybe the county is right, but there's no way the community is well served with one set of rules for smoking in the city limits, another outside the city. We ought to have some consistency.

We've set up a structure that works best when there's no controversy and you don't need a decision. In today's world, with emergencies and a changing economy, you need quick decisions and it means a single decision-maker. It works better than multiple decision-makers. Sometimes you need to make a decision quickly.

## Cast of characters:

**Charlie Belch**—Long-time local Democratic party official, he lost to Helmke for mayor in 1991

**Dan Heath and Jill Long**—Heath served as Helmke's campaign manager and chief adviser; lost to Jill Long for 4th District U.S. Representative in 1989. Long, meanwhile, was defeated by U.S. Rep. Mark Souder in 1994

**Peter Rusthoven and John Price**—Indianapolis lawyers, they lost to Helmke in the GOP primary election for U.S. Senate in 1998

# FIGHTING CRIMINALS

Problems with the Fort Wayne Police Department were a major issue in my campaign for mayor in 1987.

*Photo by Steve Linsenmayer*

### A new way of old policing

A lineup of gleaming, new, take-home police cars typified what community-oriented policing (COPS), a Helmke administration trademark, was all about: maximum visibility from police coupled with nontraditional crime-fighting techniques that enlisted help from neighborhoods. Critics, however, saw COPS as little more than public relations fluff.

Cops were unhappy with the city administration at the time, whether it was Chief Dave Riemen or Win Moses Jr. It was a concern that had emanated from the police officers themselves.

The public was sensitive to it as well. Things weren't going well, especially with some high-profile criminal cases.

And crack cocaine had come to town. There were different theories on how it had gotten here. Crack was on a different crime-fighting level. It was easy to make and transport; relatively cheap and lucrative; and very addictive to the user. As a result, you had good continuing business.

Around 1985 or 1986, a situation was occurring that was leading to more drug use in town and more crime as a result. When deals like these go bad, you see shootings and execution-style killings.

But in 1987, you had zero drug raids; the vice and narcotics squad was just four officers.

## Meeting the challenge

After the election, my top priority was choosing a police command that would have respect of the officers and beefing up narcotics and the vice squad to tackle the crack situation. And I was committed to getting more officers on board. The department in 1987 was under 300 officers, although a class was sworn in at end of year to bring it to 315. Still, it was pretty thinly staffed.

Equipment was in pretty bad shape; it had been a campaign issue as well. There were police cars with 150,000, 160,000, 170,000 miles. In addition to those concerns, police were in five different locations—City-County Building, Murray Street, Southgate, Marketplace of Canterbury, and the academy.

I chose Neil Moore as chief. I had a lot of confidence in him, not because I knew him, but he had a good reputation with officers and would help correct some of the problems with the bad perceptions from the Riemen administration. He was someone who also was working on the department's accreditation, and following changes other police departments were trying.

## Vice and narcotics

First thing we did was bring vice and narcotics to a deputy chief level within the Police Department, and put about 24 officers in it.

We started with the prosecutor and sheriff's offices to do a crackdown on drugs. It was the first major visible thing we dealt with; it was around the third week of January. It got a lot of attention because an individual was killed in the drug raid, making it big news. We even started to get some phone calls to the police from informants wanting to turn in others. Maybe they realized there was a change in the way police and government were doing business when it came to crime-fighting. Maybe they wanted to get out of the business, finger someone else in the business or maybe they wanted to make sure nobody came in with guns a'blazing at their place.

The drug raids changed the equation; we tried to raise the cost of doing business for drug dealers.

In that first year, we had 25-26 drug raids and they expanded as we went on.

## Modernizing

One of the other early issues dealt with settling disputes with minorities. There was a pending lawsuit that was still around regarding promotions; there had been a lot of issues over 10 years with the relative lack of promotions and recruitment of minority officers.

We tried to get those issues straightened out, especially since I always believed you needed a strong department that represented the entire community and that the commitment showed in the police command. It's one of the reasons in the initial command we had two African-American officers—Dave Coleman who had been a deputy chief under Moses, as well as Al Pruitt. Partly, it was a sign we wanted to deal with these issues, and to have the department in strong shape.

We also wanted to lay the groundwork for the future. Moore and I were interested in the concept of community-oriented policing. While the concept was relatively new, it also was relatively old. It was what police used to do before there were police cars and before radios came around in the 1920s. It was one of the newer ideas Neil knew a lot about; he and some of his folks looked at what was being done in Flint, Mich., and Kansas City, as far as storefront offices and bicycle patrols. We had a lot of talk early on about how to move toward community-oriented policing and break down the barriers between officers and neighborhoods.

## A new way of old policing

We opened a couple storefront offices; we decided not to close the one at the Marketplace of Canterbury. The north-side precinct had a number of problems: Officers didn't like it and it wasn't in a high-crime area at all.

We closed Marketplace of Canterbury but looked elsewhere; one on Anthony Boulevard and Pontiac Street, others at Oaklawn Court and Precious Blood School. These ended up not being the model we followed, but they were a starting point toward getting more police in the community.

Those efforts continued the entire 12 years. They went from storefront offices to a citizens' police academy to bicycle patrols and more emphasis on mounted patrols; the Target 2000 program, named after our aim to have community-oriented policing in place by 2000; new police districts; and area partnerships with neighborhood liaison officers. Even community-oriented government was an outgrowth of the COPS effort.

What sold me on COPS? It's a concept I believed in strongly, especially when I got active nationally and heard what other communities were trying to do. There were a number of parts to it. Getting police more into the community, it addressed the broken windows theory. It's the idea that if a broken window appears, pretty soon you get graffiti on the house and the house becomes a drug house, and then the whole neighborhood comes down. It's part of the idea that if you spot problems early, you can keep bigger problems from occurring.

Another part of the concept was police with open lines of communication with neighbors, allowing them to see problems directly. And part of it was just seeing and talking to a real live police officer. Part of the change from the 1920s to the 1980s, when you gave everybody a car and radio to make it easier to cover the town, took away from that intimate level of policing.

**An old yearbook**

Someone sent me a Police Department yearbook from 1935. It's fascinating. The letter from the chief touted great new advances in policing, likes cars and radios and fingerprinting. One thing that struck me about those advances from the 1920s and '30s is they really caused less face-to-face contact with people.

Thus, community-oriented policing helped combine what was good from the old way of policing with modern techniques. It found ways for officers to walk a beat, be on a bike or on a horse, be in a storefront or attend a neighborhood meeting. Any of those things helped break down the barriers and made it easier for police to serve the community. And if you spot problems early, you get leads on the bad influences in a neighborhood.

When you talk about COPS, you talk about community being part of policing. It means neighbors taking some responsibility for making their community safe. Whether it was crime watch programs, or taking back the night, it made citizens play a role.

You can never have enough police or ask them to be everywhere. You can never have, or want, police on every corner. Most crime occurs indoors where nobody's going to see it. You need citizens to police themselves and police the neighborhood. It's not vigilantism, but it means spotting problems early.

**Free time**

We decided the best way to measure this, is to look at the officers' time. We had a situation where short-staffing and crack cocaine resulted in an explosion in the number of calls for service. And there were more calls than we could possibly handle; we figured about 95 percent of an officers' time was spent responding to calls. Burglary here, accident there. They were constantly going to another call. Doing so, you couldn't do proactive things.

So we tried to restructure government and add enough personnel where eventually only 50 percent of officers' time would be spent responding to calls and the other 50 percent proactively involved in crime prevention. We tried to look at the Fire Department model. One of the reasons we've had fewer fatalities is we've put a lot of emphasis on fire prevention. The same wasn't true with crime prevention until now.

Did we see evidence of the community becoming a part of the solution? We saw it at different levels. The citizens' crime watch, for example, was around for some time, but maybe not the model that worked the best. We tried to strengthen it, but tried other models as well, like working with neighborhood associations. When folks saw things developing early, like rowdy kids throwing rocks at windows or picking on other kids, we would try to figure out ways to deal with it. It applied to rowdy kids, drug houses, motorists cutting through neighborhoods to get around a traffic intersection.

You had to have enough confidence in residents wanting to keep their neighborhoods safe and sound. With empowerment, they'd pass along tips to the police command and eventually to a liaison officer so the city could address those problems.

Over the years, with neighborhood walks and with community-oriented government, I saw a lot of crime-fighting being strengthened. The mood changed from a lot of griping and complaining, "We never see a cop in our neighborhood"-type of thing, to "We got a problem and let's find a solution."

## Resources

You can have great plans and models, but you need the resources to back them up. There were things we could do with police to make their time more useful, and some were controversial. For example, we wanted to educate people how police worked. Having police come out didn't do much unless people knew how to spot a good suspect. Also, a phone service where people could call in things like stolen bicycles allowed police to deal with more important crimes.

Bike patrols were controversial as well. We had a deputy chief, Greg Lewis, who resigned because Neil was looking at articles about bike patrols and Greg believed that wasn't the way things were done. Where Greg was coming from, I understand. But when the goal was to get officers to stop and talk with somebody, officers on bikes were better than in cars. The goal was to redistribute time to give police more citizen contact.

That could only go so far; more officers meant you had to pay for them with budget increases. In 12 years, the budget went from $10 million to $30 million, and obviously, the money came from taxpayers. People still complain the percentage of money for the parks has gone down. The reason? We put more emphasis on the policing side of things and it was appropriate. We let crime-fighting slide too long. We needed more officers to get closer to the 50 percent time for proactive policing.

## Take-home cars

We did take-home police cars for some of those same reasons. It was expensive. We had a problem before I came on board with poor equipment, with cars with too many miles. But we started our program for another reason and it was visibility. We wanted someone to see a police car whenever they were out, and I believe people do so now.

Eventually, I rarely heard anybody complain they didn't see a car in their neighborhood. If they didn't see a police car in their neighborhood, they weren't watching. I kept my eye out and generally, if you were out driving, you'd see one. A reason? We have maybe three times as many police cars as we used to. We went from 24 take-home cars, and a number of pool cars, to 240 take-home cars in the time I was mayor. Those cars were parked in driveways, were driven to and from work, and driven off-hours. So even when the officer wasn't on the clock, you'd see a car. And most times you saw a car, you didn't know if the officer was on the clock or not. It wasn't just seeing the car in the driveway, it was seeing that officer driving home or driving to the store.

It helped response times, because one of the requirements was if an officer was off the clock, they had to respond if they were the closest car to an accident or crime. Old complaints of it taking an hour for police to get to an accident also diminished because response times went down significantly as a result of more cars in service.

These were expensive programs, but they helped increase police visibility and the philosophy of community-oriented government: Police are somebody and somebody you can work and communicate with.

### Homicides

So, how did this jibe with record number of homicides in mid-1990s? Crime rates aren't directly controlled by what government does. Whenever we had falling crime rates, Moore and Hannaford cautioned me not to take credit for them going down, as we shouldn't be blamed for when crime was going up.

The increase in homicides was serious in this community. We got to all-time highs, about 42, in the mid-1990s. This was at a stage when we weren't as fully staffed as I would have liked and when we started to push some of the crucial programs in crime-fighting, like take-home cars. We also pushed the Crime Bill at the federal level, which got Fort Wayne $2 million and 30 officers.

We kept having classes, but we kept having resignations, and the one-time infusion of federal money helped us move up. When we did an analysis of it locally, we found 75 percent to 85 percent of the crime was drug-related, and it was crack cocaine still hanging around. Crack had taken a hold; we were fighting back but only staying even with the proliferation of crack houses. We'd close them down, and they'd open up somewhere else.

When they got more lucrative, folks got nastier protecting their turf. I've told people, unless you are in the drug trade or in a bad domestic situation, you most likely have little chance of being a homicide victim.

Our response was to push even harder for more take-home cars and officers. We tried Operation Strike Out in the early 1990s, a targeted anti-drug street crime team. We tried the CAN team, which was an anti-narcotics effort. These initiatives also tried to determine where drugs were being sold and used undercover agents before sending in uniformed officers.

Homicides would go up, then go down. In my last year in office, we had the lowest crime rate since about 1974. It shows some things we were doing were on the right track.

**Lines of defense**

Government is the third line of fighting crime. It's the individual who plays the most important role. The reason most people don't commit crimes is they have a sense of what's right and what's wrong. When that sense of values, that sense of right and wrong is weaker, you're going to have more crime. It's not something government controls.

The second line of defense is the family, someone who reinforces good behavior and discourages bad behavior. It doesn't have to be the family or an extended family; it could be a peer group or neighborhood as well. And that's where community policing is important. It's where the neighborhood has a sense of values enforced unofficially that encourages good behavior.

Part of what you try to get across to people, in the case where there's prostitutes in a neighborhood, is it just isn't enough for police to arrest them or run them out. Instead, you need neighborhoods doing their own policing.

For example, at St. Patrick's Catholic Church on Harrison Street, where there was an increase in prostitution, we worked with the church and the neighborhood association to really try to take back the corners from the hookers. It's something where you need government to step in, but neighbors actively working as well.

Police don't come until the third line. The individual and the family, are more important.

### Strengthening lines of defense

I tried not only to strengthen the government side, but strengthen the second level—the neighborhoods. The faith community, for example, was better at the first level. If the two levels before government were weakened, it was tougher for the police to do their job. But where those first two lines of defense were strong, you didn't have a problem.

Nobody wonders how many fires there were but how we responded to the fire. With the police, it wasn't how long it took them to respond to crime, but to blame them if the crime had occurred. And it never totally made sense to me. Fire departments don't start fires, but respond to them. Police don't start crimes, but also respond to them.

Meanwhile, you get criticized how you respond to crime as well. It's a tricky business. There were some problems we should have seen coming but didn't handle as well as we should have. We had done some of the early targeted drug work—Operation Strike Out, the Community Anti-Narcotics, or CAN, Team, for example. But part of what we also did is lay early groundwork with neighborhoods and ministers, so when we would do something new in crime-fighting, we had more institutional support in the community.

But later on, as crime started to escalate in the mid-1990s, we didn't do that as well.

### Complaints pop up

Part of it was the pressure to respond to the large number of calls. We started to get posturing from the Sheriff's Department where it would come in to an area and do police work without laying any groundwork, and we felt that wasn't necessary.

At the same time, we were hiring a lot of officers. One of the dangers with new hires is that you don't have officers fully attuned to community policing, with a sensitivity to the community. We realized the pitfalls ahead of time and I thought we were doing fairly well in the selection process. But in retrospect, when we had the Crime Bill class, we almost added too quickly to the Police Department with large classes. Actually, some of our problems were with lateral transfers from other police jurisdictions than with our own rookie hires.

Adding many officers quickly changed the culture of the Police Department. Suddenly, you were seeing more in the community, and those officers were reading about the crime rates going up, and they wanted to do something to stop it. As a result, there was less supervision, mentoring and training over officers than had been in the past. And there were some officers with too much of a "cowboy attitude" about things.

It's a fine line. You want aggressive policing, you want to fight the bad guys, but you also want to be sure you are following the law and the Constitution, and treating people with respect.

### New cops/old outlook

It's a tough situation. From the officers' perspective, especially if they're new and under pressure, there's an attitude where everyone is seen as the bad guy and you always have to be watching yourself. And the slightest bit of confrontation can escalate.

Once this started to occur and I started to hear more examples, we did things early on I thought would help. For example, we had a citizens contact office where people could file complaints without having to go to the police station. It was a bit of a challenge to explain to them the internal affairs department wasn't the only avenue to address grievances. You could get a lawyer, go to the prosecutor or the U.S. Attorney for remedies.

I always stressed the police and I didn't want bad cops, and if there were some, we supported appropriate discipline. To do that, we needed information. But by the time we were getting information, we had a few too many folks causing problems.

At the same time, Chief Neil Moore was seen in the community as not being as sensitive to the complaints. Neil was always concerned but there was an impression he wasn't. Neil made the decision on his own it was time to go. He wasn't forced out, but it was probably time. Neil was somebody who was always supportive of the Police Department and sometimes needed to be tougher in terms of discipline.

### Problems with the minority community

Dan Hannaford, who was a strong part of Neil's administration, really scored points for himself when he appeared at a meeting at Greater Progressive Baptist Church after some of the tensions were at their highest.

Hannaford, as assistant chief, was there, and showed he and the department were sensitive to the complaints.

Going to the U.S. Justice Department with complaints about alleged police mistreatment of minorities—as a group of minority ministers did—however, doesn't do a whole heck of a lot. In this case, the Justice Department didn't really do anything. It pretty much felt we were taking care of the issue on our own. If we hadn't, the Justice Department would have stepped in. Going to the Justice Department was the ministers' way of saying there's a growing problem, and it sent a message to the broader community there's a serious problem. And I agreed. There was a serious problem that had to be dealt with. It was a way for ministers to legitimately raise issues.

We had started working with the ministers before that day to find ways to help the situation. Hannaford coming on sent a sign there were going to be some changes. Dan took a stricter view on discipline; at least the perception as stricter than Neil. We put in a whole new police command and it was not a slam against the folks who were there. But it sent a message we needed new folks with new ideas. They communicated closely with Payne Brown and I to work with the minority community to bring things on track. And I think we did.

**Task force**

One of the most important things we did is put together a forum on police-community relations. The balanced task force brought a lot of good proposals, like video cameras on the cars to protect police and citizens and more authority for line officers to discipline others.

Anytime you have 390 individuals, regardless of profession, you're going to get a few that cause problems. And it's the few who caused problems that gave the department a bad image. It's a tough situation. We want police to be aggressive, but not too aggressive. We want police to protect us from the bad guys, but people don't normally have clear identifiable tags that say, "I'm a good guy, I'm a bad guy." For most of us, being the bad guy means running the stop sign or exceeding the speed limit. But most of the time the officer doesn't know what he or she is facing, and our efforts through the task force gave us a lot stronger department.

We also made changes in training and in the academy to keep an eye on whom we select, how we train and how we discipline.

Those challenges continue. In the campaign of 1999, between Linda Buskirk and Graham Richard, we were criticized for not hiring fast enough even though we had a full class of 26 starting in July. Mayor Richard had an idea of a different way to get new officers in there right away. And I cautioned him if you put people in there too quickly, either with a lateral transfer or a quicker training period, you run the risk of problems.

For example, with lateral classes, we believed it would be a great idea to bring in other officers who had experience and training, and who wouldn't need that much training time. Instead, we found they were leaving from other departments because of problems there.

I tried to do all I could—in light of criticism that I was racially insensitive—to show I wouldn't countenance any racial discrimination in my administration and in the way we did business. The leaders of the minority community believed me and had confidence in my attitude. They realized it was not always easy to get those working for you to be of the same mind. Part of the reason we were successful in keeping potentially explosive situations from getting worse was the good relationship I had with leaders in the minority community like the Revs. Ternae Jordan and Mike Nickleson and local NAACP President Liz Dobynes. I was always willing to listen, talk and make changes.

## Open lines of communication

Communication is important. When watching other cities, you notice police/community relations turn out tense when elected leaders and community leaders only talk through the media or in antagonistic situations. I tried to speak with the black and Hispanic communities on a regular basis, so when things were bad, I knew how to get hold of them and they knew how to get hold of me.

Meanwhile, my job was to select a chief, and I worked with Hannaford and Moore in selecting the top slots. Outside of that, I relied on them to do crime-fighting, to look at major initiatives like take-home cars. I wanted to be involved with those initiatives, but how specific crime was being handled, it was a police job. My job was to help set the broad direction, the tenor of how we did business, to help get the resources there to do it, including good people to carry it out. They did the actual crime-fighting.

I'd hear enough from citizens about specific cases, and I passed them on to the chief to check on. It also let the chief know there was an issue to make sure it wasn't indicative of a broader problem. And it showed we weren't ignoring a specific crime or a specific area, or that we had a rogue officer we needed to take care of.

## The ugly side of life

I also got exposed to the ugly side of life in Fort Wayne. Talking with officers, you got details of what's happening undercover or behind the scenes. It's pretty clear it's a grizzly, messy business. One thing was clear to me; it takes a special kind of person to be a police officer. I couldn't do it. You have a lot of challenges and pressures an ordinary citizen never sees. I always was impressed and proud of the efforts of nearly all our officers. They're good men and women who did tough jobs. People are always trying to play games with you and cut corners, when some of the situations you'd see were beyond the comprehension of ordinary people. You get a different view of life from there.

There's the challenge from the other side as well. There's the risk of getting jaded. If all you see is the bad side of the community, you are going to start making mistakes. But if you work with community and neighborhood folks who want to make life better, it really helps reinforce that most people are good people. And it helps police carry on.

**Mean streets**

Were there neighborhoods with persistent crime problems worth giving up on? Not really, because I walked most of them. I walked streets where the chief or someone else would tell me later, "Boy, that's some of the toughest streets in town, or where there's the most drug houses."

Walking 4-5 p.m. and knocking on doors, you saw bad houses and people who looked rough, but people generally were positive. There were people who cared, despite locks on their doors, security systems and them peeking from windows. It gave me faith most people were good even on the toughest and meanest streets. There was some hope. A house or two in some of these areas were the only ones causing problems and terrorizing the neighborhood. If we could just find a way to deal with the isolated problem we could help the neighborhood. The catch was if you made progress on one street, criminals would move to another. Or a gang leader would take over the mantle of the guy we had just arrested or the guy who had just gotten killed.

Often, a single person or two affected the crime rate in an entire neighborhood. There were times when we had a person locked up, the crime rate would fall, and as soon as he got out, it would go back up again. One or two individuals drive a lot of crime. It would be great if we knew who they were, but the tricky problem with fighting crime, despite knowing who these people are, knowing it and being able to prove it are two different things. The situation's the source of a lot of frustration in neighborhoods.

We couldn't shut down "known" drug houses without undercover buys we could take to the prosecutor. The court's level of proof is different than people's level of knowing.

## A barometer of success

What was the barometer of success? We looked at different statistics, both overall and of serious crimes. We would poll on an annual basis about safety in neighborhoods. We spoke with neighborhoods, with area partnerships and their officers, to give us a sense if we were making progress.

Then there was Tom Ostrognai, a local landlord, who videotaped suspected drug houses. He aired them on Channel 10, to show the alleged drug deals going on. He called it something like Drug Wars.

The catch is just because you can get a video camera of somebody knocking on a door on a regular basis and handing something to another person, without an undercover buy or an arrest right away, the video couldn't get anybody convicted. We tried different tactics of stationing cars at some areas of a neighborhood to disrupt traffic. But, do you want to disrupt traffic so it moves elsewhere or do you want to make an arrest?

## I make a drug buy

Early on, Ostrognai wanted me to see drug buys in person. He had a property on Chestnut Street and this was where he had filmed some of his videos. It was a cold winter day, and we were bundled up quite a bit. I didn't want to look mayoral or visible, so I guess I had jeans on.

We went to this house and looked out a window, trying to observe drug buys. This is the sort of stuff he had on this TV show. We did this for about one or two hours and not a single thing happened. It shows part of the challenge for police—staking out where nothing is happening.

Tom was frustrated that nothing was happening, and I was cold. So we went driving around, and he was going to show me drug deals while cruising. It was about 4 p.m., and he pointed out somebody he believed was selling drugs. I said, "Are you sure about that?" It's probably what's happening but you can never be sure.

We drive up to this one place, and he wants me to try to make a crack buy. I'm concerned about breaking the law, but I also want to see what's going on here. So we drive up to this place, and I don't look like I'm in disguise, but I don't have a coat or tie on either. I rolled down the window, and just did hand signals to this guy because I didn't want to entrap anybody. And some guy brings over a rock of something, and I hand over $20—maybe it was Ostognai's, maybe it was mine. I basically bought some stuff from this guy with a school bus half a block in front of us. It really showed how easy it was to buy drugs.

We went straight to the Police Department and told them where we bought it so they could go right out. By the time they got there, nobody was around. It was crack cocaine. The incident showed you could buy this stuff. It showed me that a lot of folks buying this stuff were white folks from non-poor neighborhoods in town who pull up in a pickup like I did with Ostrognai and very quickly get a rock or two of crack. It was obvious we had problems.

Ostrognai, meanwhile, couldn't believe I did this. "You don't have a gun on you, you don't have anything," he said. Instead, my attitude was that I'm trusting of people so let's see what happens.

Then I told him I didn't want to talk about the incident too much publicly; he's mentioned it a couple of times afterward, but not too publicly.

## Frustrations

It shows how fighting crime is frustrating. That situation showed it. I bought drugs but unless I was an undercover police officer who could make an arrest, it was too late by the time the cops got there.

Despite who buys drugs, the reality is that drugs are sold outwardly in some areas more than others. A lot of what happens, drugs could be sold in one part of town but people come from all parts of town to buy them. Also, they're sold in people's basements and behind closed doors. It's different with visible sales, or with street prostitution—those criminals are easier to arrest.

Bigger drug deals could be happening in private offices and behind closed doors in any part of town, more so than on the street. But you're not seeing it.

The kinds of crimes that cause problems in the community are everywhere. But the kinds of crimes that especially bring down a neighborhood are the ones that are visible, and isolated in certain parts of town.

You need flexibility to deal with these problems. I found out over the years, whenever we tried something new, the bad guys also tried something new. So we had to change our tactics whenever they changed theirs. You just keep doing it.

## A poor relationship

The evolution of the poor city-county police relationship was frustrating. Tensions went back up sometimes, whether over differing pay scales or differing backgrounds, or the kinds of problems they were dealing with. In some communities, city cops see the county cops as more of the rural types, the "County Mountie" derogatory stereotype. These tensions go both ways.

A lot of the problem started to occur with the personalities of the different sheriffs. When Dan Figel was sheriff during my first term, we had a pretty good relationship; so did Chief Neil Moore and I. Part of the problem started with the sheriff's election to succeed Figel in 1990. A large part of it goes back to the GOP primary election, when one of our city deputies, Pat Harper, ran against Joe Squadrito. And Harper, while deputy chief, was not my candidate. My father might have been on Squadrito's election team. It was something that clearly had potential for problems. But I wasn't directly involved.

The campaign also got messy. Squadrito's opponent in the November election, Democrat Glen Harpel, accused the department of mishandling a shooting in a January 1988 joint drug operation. There were accusations, with no basis, about Martin Clay Carter, believed to be a high-volume cocaine dealer, being executed when police busted into the Lewis Street house he was in.

These accusations evoked suspicion of the city's involvement, although I did not know from where the accusations came.

I'd known Squadrito for some time, and I had early meetings with him in hope of working as well with him as Figel. The relationship, however, always seemed a bit tense. I don't know if it was my fault or Joe's fault, but from my perspective it always was a bit tense.

## Joe, the Federalist Papers and I

Early on, I remember having Squadrito up to my office to talk about things. It wasn't long before I believed he was lecturing me about the Federalist Papers and his theories of limited government. Maybe I read the situation wrong but I didn't like being lectured to by anybody, Squadrito included. I'd been a political science major and I studied the Federalist Papers. This wasn't an area I was unfamiliar with. I know the Federalist Papers and what they contain.

I don't mind having good spirited discussions and disagreements with anybody. But early on there were tensions there, and they seemed to escalate during Joe's eight years in office.

During the 1995 city election, there was talk Joe was going to run for mayor. There had been criticisms of the city's drug-fighting efforts. He had been critical of Neil Moore publicly. It didn't lead to good relationships with Neil Moore, the Police Department or me. As we faced challenges with the drug situation, I and the city Police Department sensed Joe was out there second-guessing a lot of things we were doing.

Part of it was our move toward community-oriented policing. The challenges were, oftentimes, if you went to community-oriented policing too quickly and shoved it at officers without their buy-in, they would be resistant and would talk with Joe. This would feed in to his ideas the city was getting too soft. There was an attitude this stuff was too soft; all we needed was some hardheaded, "knock-their-heads-around" mentality.

It started to come across in public comments. Here we're taking a long, two-year process to get our Target 2000 community policing effort by teaming up officers who were resistant to change with those who helped draw up the program. Instead, the dissension brought up the argument that officers don't want to be social workers, especially at times when it looks like crime is going up.

All these tensions: Between Joe and I, Neil and Joe. There's mistrust over the Harper situation. There's political considerations with Joe having an eye on the mayor's office. There's talk that since the crime rate outside the city is low, Squadrito is doing a great job. And since the crime rate inside the city is worse, Fort Wayne is doing a lousy job. All these things made it difficult for us to work together.

## Other problems

There were other problems. There was a joint program, a regional anti-drug task force with the U.S. Attorney's Office, the State Police and the prosecutor, that the sheriff and city were involved in. Joe didn't want to be part of any joint programs and left it.

I still remember one meeting when George Bush was president. There were "weed and seed" funds. You could get grants, part of which would "weed" out crime, and part of which would "seed" proactive efforts. We had a meeting early on with the prosecutor, the sheriff and our folks to send in our application. It was around 1992. We had this whole meeting about what should the boundaries be, what should we put in this application. After meeting for half an hour or more, Joe starts to walk out. Somebody said, "We're going to need you to put your signature on this form." And he basically said, "I'm not signing anything."

He hadn't raised one word of criticism during the entire meeting, but just basically said he wasn't going to sign a joint application on anything. It made it really hard to do things together with that kind of attitude.

When I was out lobbying for the Federal Crime Bill, Joe would show up at these White House meetings, and then come back and say, "This is disgusting. This is the wrong approach. We don't need these things." He said he'd gotten other invitations from the White House and he turned down those. It was when Clinton became president; it was a bit of a slap at me and the allegations I was a bit too friendly with Clinton.

## The dynamic

Sometimes, Joe was just tough to work with. He would announce some unilateral program where he was going to go in and save the southeast side of the city. He did it with Councilman Cletus Edmonds' support.

He would just go in, and first of all, it would drive our folks nuts. They weren't sure what was going on, where county police were going to be. Particularly with drug dealing, if we're doing an undercover operation some place, we didn't want the county sheriff's people to do a drug raid on a house where we had agents inside. We could have been working on a long-range deal not just to get the house but the supplier, and then, all of a sudden, you can get some real problems with the sheriff's people coming in with our undercover people in there.

We had several situations that came close to happening, or had happened, because Joe didn't want to share information. Meanwhile, Joe believed we had some bad officers who couldn't be trusted. My point was, if we have a problem, tell me whom they are and we'll try to get rid of them. Over the last few years, we had found officers who were involved in some shady stuff.

The relationship between us always was more adversary, more political, with more posturing than necessary.

There were times when Joe was going to go in and save the south side with targeted policing. Joe went before TV cameras and they went with him. He's in the car the first night, and the TV stations are reporting it. But the fact is, he never went back the next night and his people never did either. It was all for PR. But everybody assumed that Joe and his people were in there for weeks afterward.

I had concerns with those early county police forays on the southeast side of Fort Wayne. I remember being at a meeting at one of the black churches trying to work on our neighborhood programs. I was driving back home, down Rudisill Boulevard around 10 p.m. in the summertime. All of a sudden, I passed a stop sign on one of the side streets on East Rudisill. There, I saw a sheriff's car had stopped somebody and a deputy with a shotgun or some large rifle held across his chest was looking out at all the cars driving on Rudisill. I felt intimidated. If I felt intimidated, a public figure, how did the poor or minority person driving down the street feel?

Part of that approach was intimidation. It meant you come in with the guns out and the big, burly guys ready to shoot—at least it was the impression—at any incident, or stop any car that looked suspicious. And that's the stuff I sensed ended up causing more problems fighting crime. Instead, you have to fight crime in ways folks aren't harassed.

## The gall of it all

One of the other things that galled us—and it's part of the structural nature of the sheriff's department—is that as a city resident, you pay the same amount for the sheriff's department as folks in the suburbs. But the sheriff, except for these special cases, never did anything inside the city.

As a result, city taxpayers would subsidize the sheriff's department, and the sheriff would always act like he was doing the city a favor by spending other folks' money to solve our problem. But it was our money that helped pay for the sheriff.

Another galling aspect? The sheriff's responsibility is to serve warrants countywide, inside and outside the city. It's not the job of city police to serve warrants. We were at a stage where there was a backlog of 10,000-12,000 warrants that hadn't been served inside the city. We always felt that if the sheriff just did his job and served these warrants, it would take care of the problem more than the posturing and playing to the media and the "big, tough guy stuff" to help reduce crime.

If you get people who have outstanding warrants—whether it's for failing to pay parking tickets or not showing up at a court hearing—and get them off the street, or at least back to take care of their warrants, the community would be in better shape.

## Some cooperation

We would work on some efforts together. We did a Metro Squad together, leading to the mayor's election in 1995. It's at a time Squadrito is making noises about running for mayor, and Allen County GOP Chairman Steve Shine tried to bring us together at a dinner, just the three of us. We all smoked cigars and drank cognac afterward. It was one of these, "How can we work together? How can we make peace with all our problems?" kind of get-togethers.

Indicating he had some proposals, one of them was the Metro Squad he'd be in charge of but where I and the Police Department would have some say and our people would communicate what was going on. We tried it around 1995, and it did some decent things but never really worked as well as it should have, part of it being the intrinsic jealousies and turf battles.

We tried to do some things together but it wasn't easy.

## The Klan

When we had the first Ku Klux Klan rallies in front of the courthouse, we worked well together. I spent most of the afternoon in the sheriff's office, with Joe and Neil watching things. We had good advance planning and the execution worked out well. It showed we could work together.

But the next year, it showed how we couldn't work together when the Klan came back. That same weekend, I was going to be in Washington for a U.S. Conference of Mayors meeting, and it was going to be some lousy, 20-below-zero weather. When I discussed it with Neil and our people, they believed the weather would be of help because it would cut down on the number of Klan people and the crowd. It made for the perfect situation, making the situation easier to control.

However, the sheriff didn't want to be part of policing the rally because he didn't want his men to be cold. The cold was a threat to their safety. It turned out to be a situation where he said he wasn't going to be a part of the rally but we went ahead anyway and handled it very well.

Then Joe was out later saying we were chicken. If anything, he was the chicken. He didn't want to be out in the cold. Instead, we were chicken because we wouldn't cancel the event, he said.

It never made sense.

## Nonsensical policing

He was a tough guy to deal with and part of it really showed up after Joe left office and Jim Herman became sheriff. Herman had been his deputy and somebody Squadrito endorsed, but just in that first year, 1999, the relationship between the city and county got better right away. It showed again how individual personalities in these elected positions can make or break cooperation.

It just doesn't make sense to have two police agencies covering the same jurisdiction. In effect, while the city's jurisdiction doesn't extend beyond Fort Wayne's boundary line, the sheriff is within the city, at least when it comes to the jail, warrants and special law enforcement techniques. With two departments, they better work together well or they're going to step on each other's toes and cause problems.

For me, it begs the larger question. Why do we have this kind of setup? The bad guys don't organize themselves that way. Burglary rings or drug selling gangs don't treat things differently inside or outside the city limits. It's not the most efficient way to fight crime with these arbitrary boundary lines.

It would make a lot more sense with a combined, joint law enforcement agency. You can elect a chief, like the sheriff, or have him appointed by the mayor, like in the city. Do you really want the sheriff to have the broad range of responsibilities? Or maybe he should just be the jailer and let police agencies do the rest.

It doesn't make sense now; it worked well when personalities worked well, but not when personalities didn't mesh.

## The public suffers

Regardless of personalities, it's the public that's going to suffer when you have clashing personalities, duplication and two people trying to raid the same drug house without knowing who's undercover in there.

## Soft on crime? Hardly.

I can't understand how anyone could say we were soft on crime. The emphasis we put on crime-fighting belies the characterization. We increased the budget from $10 million to $30 million, and it wasn't easy. We got more fully staffed, to 390 officers; we got take-home police cars; we established a centralized police station; we put video cameras and mobile data terminals in cars; and we started a whole new technique of policing.

We made fighting crime and public safety the No. 1 emphasis of our administration.

How do you judge if you're successful? Sometimes statistics don't show a complete, or accurate, picture. But in 1999, crime numbers show total crime down the most since 1974. And if it's the measure, we're doing well.

Anybody who suffers from crime, however, will feel we've done badly. We looked at different measures: total crime rate, total number of crimes, amount of police being proactive, the number of crimes solved, for example, to figure out how we were doing.

I felt safe going into any part of the community at any time. Perception, however, plays a big role. People read the headlines, and over-generalize their conclusions from it. A lot of crime isn't random, it's related to drugs or gang activity. The random ones get most of the headlines and are of concern.

But most crimes aren't random acts. Look at stolen cars: 75 percent of those we analyzed one year had the keys in them or the motor running when they were stolen.

## Tools

We believed community-policing would be a tool that would work here. Target 2000 was the name we put on one of our early grant applications to the federal government to help fund the initiative. It was turned down. The aim was to have community-oriented policing in place by 2000. We wanted it for the entire community, and all officers to be involved. Other places would do it in certain neighborhoods only; we wanted it as a philosophy that was embraced by the entire community. As a result, the effort had to be long-range.

A lot of police, we believed, would be resistant to the approach. The approach wasn't just to respond to high-profile crime, but look at situations that contribute to crime. We had a committee of about 35 people, and worked for two years, through about 1994-95, looking at how other communities did its COPS programs. Some of the officers on the group were very much against the new approach. Capt. George Letz, for example, had the attitude, "We don't need this." By the end of our efforts, he was one of the biggest cheerleaders for the approach.

It was a realization that a Sgt. Friday approach of "Just the facts, ma'am" wasn't working anymore. An officer needed to be closely allied, trusted and needed by the community.

Target 2000 proposed steps to break down barriers between police and community. We redrew all police districts so they didn't cross neighborhood boundary lines. We put police districts into quadrants. We created a citywide community services council. The issues in different neighborhoods often are distinct; it's why we had neighborhood liaison officers.

As a result, we created a neighborhood, quadrant and citywide level of contact for police and residents to deal with problems.

## Taking it further

COPS went beyond crime issues, and addressed the concern, "I'm a police officer, I don't want to be a social worker." It's why Code Enforcement inspectors and other city workers got involved in direct action teams to address quality-of-life issues.

The efforts helped police deal with crime before it happened and became a major issue. At first, we believed it would take a decade to institutionalize. Instead, it became successful a lot sooner, and helped the community get national recognition. And it showed you don't look at policing issues separately from others.

We needed a "front door" approach to government. Streets clear of snow where kids could play, for example, helped you feel comfortable with the neighborhood outside your front door. The whole concept of community-oriented government was aimed at those front-door issues: not those that necessarily make headlines but issues residents really care about.

This wasn't the latest fad or gimmick. Chief Moore and I believed COPS was going to be very successful and last a long time. It was returning police to the roots of policing, and correcting trends that evolved from technology.

I believe this firmly: Police won't be effective unless they have the trust of the community. And you get it through interaction and with an understanding of those specific issues of to residents. You can't have police seen as an invading force or a group that's coming in just to bang heads. We don't want a police state with officers on every corner. It's why we have to rely somewhat on the neighborhood doing a level of policing on its own, with the confidence police are doing their job when needed.

## No police state

It's why I opposed random car stops. When we talk about crime, we think about policing aimed at the bad guys, so they're the ones who are stopped and hassled. But we often don't stop to think it could be us, or our friends or children, who are stopped and hassled. We need to look at the system overall. Random traffic stops are wrong as policy. It's not appropriate to stop every 10th car, for example, because such stops bring us a step closer to a police state.

I saw firsthand what those random searches could do.

I was driving to Bloomington one evening, and south of Indy, I saw all sorts of police lights on U.S. 37. Being a divided highway, I believed it was a big accident. When I came closer, I saw it was just police pulling over cars, maybe after the 10th or 15th car. And you could tell it would be 30 minutes, maybe even 45 minutes, and not a quick process, before getting past the roadblock.

I kept driving to Bloomington and then checked the papers next day but found nothing. I was at a reunion of student body officials, and spoke about the incident with a fellow who was president a year before me who is now on the Indiana Court of Appeals. We figured out it was one of these random stops. It was hard for me, a lawyer, to accept such an activity could be legal. We need to look at these things and ask, "What if it was me? It's late at night, I'm tired and want to get to bed, with a busy schedule next day. I don't have any drugs and I haven't been drinking, and have no guns in my car."

But just because of this policy, I could be pulled over and detained for some time; it's still an intrusion into my freedom. While government has a balancing role, without specific reason to believe something illegal was happening, it didn't make sense to me.

I started to raise this issue with others: Is it legal? All of a sudden, I hear it's being done in Indy and could be coming to Fort Wayne. And I said, no way. I don't like this and we weren't going to do it.

## A bad message

Such random stops send a very negative message about the government's role in our lives. Police could do a more efficient job if they could get into people's homes and check their cars for drugs and other illegalities. But we'd be giving up a lot of our rights and freedoms. You have to keep things in balance. And part of my job as mayor was to do that.

Police technically can stop someone because their blinker isn't working properly. But if not used carefully, it isn't seen as a tool to protect us but a tool of a police state. You could get some arrests from it, but you turn off the entire community to a police department's primary role to serve and protect.

I heard from people who were stopped because of their skin color, and that was wrong. It's something we need to fight against. One of our top CEOs in town, an African

American, spoke with me and said one of his children home from college was stopped two or three times in the course of a Christmas vacation. The child was doing nothing out of the ordinary but obviously a target because of race.

Police power is so serious. They can carry guns, stop and arrest you. They have to be careful with the power they use. As mayor, it's important you do your part to see you have a good department doing its job.

## Discipline

Anytime we disciplined an officer, we heard murmuring we were being too politically correct or didn't know policing. I believed it was important for police to understand from the community's perspective how this looked and how we needed balance. A strong department meant not only more cops and money and equipment, but one that had gotten support from the entire community.

And the support was more important than the police budget or take-home cars.

Rogue cops. It's a small number of officers who create problems, no more than five or six at one time. The goal was to find out who's causing the problem, to correct it or get rid of them. A lot of this was objected to by police as interference, but if an officer makes mistakes, there are consequences. When it happens, the challenge is to take care of it as quickly as possible. We moved swiftly in all cases, even with due process rights of individuals. Officers have rights. Even with allegations, we had to prove them before we could discipline or fire someone.

It's one of the reasons we went to a three-civilian safety board, people who are independent thinkers. Sometimes they'd agree with discipline; other times, not. It was an independent, semi-judicial group looking at these incidents.

## Legacy

Even with the new Graham Richard administration, folks seem to have bought into the philosophy of community-oriented government and policing. One of the reasons I ran for a third term was because the philosophy was too new, and thus, at risk. Four more years helped institutionalize COPS with police and residents.

It's where I believe we are now. Neighborhoods have bought into it and so have police. The general concept of community-oriented policing is here to stay and it's going to make the community safer. COPS won't make it a perfect world, but it brings together police and the community.

It's my legacy. It's something as significant and something I'm as proud of as anything else I've done. It's a change in the way people relate with city government. We've changed the way people think, and what's in their heads and hearts.

## Cast of characters:

**Neil Moore and Dan Hannaford**—Two police chiefs under Helmke

**Tom Ostrognai**—A local landlord and unsuccessful political candidate, he's made a reputation chronicling alleged drug activity in Fort Wayne neighborhoods

**Pat Harper**—A city police captain who ran unsuccessfully for Allen County Sheriff

# SEX, LIES AND BILL CLINTON

*Photo by Courtesy of Paul Helmke*

**Classroom courtroom**

Yale Law School's Barrister's Union—a group of students, including Paul Helmke, Bill Clinton and his future wife, Hillary Rodham, who took part in mock trials as part of their extracurricular studies—pose for a photo in a classroom courtroom in 1973. According to a 25th anniversary listing in 1998, they are, from left: David Golub, a Stamford, Conn., lawyer; Anthony Paul, a lawyer in Wayne, Pa.; Michael Conway, a Chicago lawyer; Rufus Cormier, a Houston, Texas, lawyer; Jeffrey Rogers, a city attorney in Portland, Ore., and the son of William Rogers, secretary of state under

President Nixon; Paul Helmke; Robert
Alsdorf, a Superior Court judge in Seattle;
Hillary Rodham; Daniel Johnson, a Palo
Alto, Calif., attorney; Bill Clinton; and Jack
Fuller, publisher of the Chicago Tribune.

On the national scene, boy did I take my hits!

Early on, I supported the so-called stimulus package offered by the
Clinton administration. It was the right thing for the community. I don't
believe people realize some of the challenges faced by the city. We used to
get a lot of federal funding for cities. It isn't like that today. The funding
programs dried up during the Reagan years.

It meant a lot less ability to access federal funds, especially compared with
the administration of previous mayors Win Moses Jr., Bob Armstrong and
Ivan Lebamoff.

I was willing to live with it, but those federal cuts came with federal mandates. In the past, the federal government said you have to fix your sewers
and gave you some money to do it. Now, Washington gives the same mandates without necessarily any federal dollars. So when Clinton pushed the
stimulus package to get money back to the cities, I jumped at the chance
because we had legitimate needs. I endorsed it. And while it was a small
part of the big budget bill, that's where battle lines were drawn.

## Stimulus package

The stimulus package, however, never came to a vote. It was held up in
the Senate and the Clinton administration withdrew it. I remember meeting with Sen. Robert Dole and mayors from other cities, asking why such
a small part of the budget was being targeted for opposition. It was a political and tactical decision to take it on because there wasn't much of a

budget constituency for cities. That's where Clinton opponents honed in the attack.

I don't apologize for the support. In retrospect, the economy got so strong, maybe it wasn't as necessary. But at the time, it surely looked like it would have helped.

I got caught up in the crosscurrents of national politics, and it led to recriminations here and statewide. The Indiana Policy Review played up a letter from Rex Early, who had been state GOP chairman, attacking me on this position. I was called Remocrat of the Year.

When I ran for U.S. Senate in 1998, folks wanted me to explain my position in support of the Clinton administration from that time. An explanation? It was the same motivation as with the federal crime bill in 1994. This had the Brady Bill aspect, with more money for police. It was a legitimate role for government to fund local law enforcement efforts. It helped us hire 30 police officers quickly, and beef up the Police Department.

**Clinton and hot buttons**

Since it was connected with Clinton and pushed hot button issues like guns, it got a lot of criticism. I was on the south lawn of the White House when the bill was signed because I had decided I was going to support this. And if I'm going to take the political heat to get it passed, I'll do my part. At the signing ceremony, another Republican who was active with the bill didn't want to be seen sitting in the front row to minimize political fallout.

Not me. In for a dime, in for a dollar.

Also that day at the podium was Bud Meeks. At the time, he was president of the national sheriffs association, who ran unsuccessfully for mayor in 1983 and was a longtime darling of the local GOP. I came back to Fort

Wayne and caught all this flak. And I think, "How can it be so bad if Bud Meeks is one of the people up there at the podium?"

The whole Brady Bill, crime bill effort led some Republicans to question my credentials, and it's been a factor in my political positions. It's interesting. I knew Clinton. I went to law school with him—I was on the Barrister's Union with him and Hillary and 12 others at Yale. I followed his career. But I was just on his mailing list, with maybe one or two friendly letters shortly after law school, not much more. The last time I had contact with him was around 1980 until he ran for president.

I believed having the president be somebody I knew would help our city. I would use it to Fort Wayne's advantage. Instead, it got everybody suspicious. A lot of people thought I was his roommate in college. No, I wasn't. I was married and lived with my wife; he lived elsewhere.

Other than at mayoral settings, I really didn't speak with him. Yet those early ties, along with the support for the crime bill and other Clinton initiatives, coupled with the Republican hatred for Clinton, really put me in the cross hairs. I've always been a Republican. I have never publicly endorsed a Democrat even when there where Republicans I didn't like and would even vote for a Democrat occasionally. Yet, I'm catching all this flak over it.

### Flak, flak and more flak

Some of the flak would be from GOP types like Rex Early, Craig Ladwig—all these conservative Indiana Policy Review types. In publications, I became one of their favorite whipping boys. Yet I had supported several good Republican themes, like strong law enforcement, empowering neighborhoods, fiscal responsibility, and I had fought for local control. These are good GOP themes, but I never got the credit.

Part of the problem, as mayor, you're looked at suspiciously by true believers, whether to the right or left. When you're mayor, it's not just about theory.

You're not voting a theoretical position. You actually have to do something. When you're in the legislative branches, you can say you're for or against something. As mayor, you can be for or against something but you still have to do it. If it doesn't work, you have to try something else. Mayors are forced to be pragmatists. The garbage has to be picked up, the fires have to be responded to and the streets need to be cleaned. You can duck it and rely on your philosophy for a short time, but your philosophy also has to deal with a real world.

All mayors of every party are attacked by their party for not being ideologically pure, for not following the straight party line. But you have to deliver. And you can't hide behind somebody else. As a legislator, you can hide behind an argument that you're in the minority, or it was a committee vote, or it was the caucus decision. When you're mayor, you can't hide behind a decision. It's just you. That's why it's hard to find mayors who move up in politics. Sen. Dick Lugar, former Indianapolis mayor, is a rare exception. You don't see many mayors who do well later on.

But the ideologically pure sometimes didn't like former Republican Indianapolis mayors Bill Hudnut, Lugar and Steve Goldsmith. So I figured I was running in good company.

## Cozying up to Clinton

It interested me that people believed I was cozying up to Clinton because I was bucking for a Washington job. I wasn't looking for something. That wasn't my agenda. Folks had a hard time otherwise understanding why I would be taking these unpopular political positions if not for my own political gain. There was something in it for me, people believed. There was political cost, so there must be personal payoff. But it's not how I do business.

A good politician can sell his belief he's doing what's right for the community. Yet people believed Helmke was endorsing these things because he could get something from Clinton. I never tried to get something; it wasn't my agenda. I wanted to be a good mayor.

## Didn't turn out so well

The relationship with Washington didn't turn out so well. Clinton's impeachment and the issue with Monica Lewinsky came up when I was on the campaign trail for U.S. Senate. I was in Terre Haute speaking to a GOP group, when somebody told me about the Monica story as it first broke out. I was curious about the details, the salacious gossip.

I was at the winter meeting of the U.S. Conference of Mayors where the subject came up, and I heard all the political news shows saying Clinton would resign soon because of it.

It was an interesting time to be in Washington. I went to the State of the Union address, and there was no mention about resigning. Rumors were flying. We had a meeting in the White House, and as president of the U.S. Conference of Mayors, I was supposed to introduce Clinton. Some of his staff weren't sure. They were concerned that as a Republican, I might take a cheap shot at Clinton. But I'm not the sort to take cheap shots, and it's not the right way to do things.

## Clinton and Monica and me

So we have a reception, and some of the mayors are in a room with Cabinet members. And Clinton comes in. Remember, this is a week full of rumors, with speculation swirling. And it's an amazing scene. He walks in, says hello to the five mayors and Cabinet members. He goes up to Bruce Babbitt, the secretary of the interior, who's been in the news as well over some controversy about improper handling of Indian casino contracts. And Babbitt looks really glum. Clinton comes over to him and said, "I did all this just to keep you off the front pages this week."

It really threw Babbitt and me. Here's Clinton joking about something that's obviously coming really close to bringing down his presidency. And he had that kind of way of handling people. It is one of his strengths and weaknesses.

The Cabinet goes out and we sit down. It's just Frederico Pena, energy secretary and former mayor of Denver, Clinton and I. The three of us are supposed to be introduced at the same time. Pena's supposed to introduce me, and I'm supposed to introduce Clinton. So we're standing there, just the three of us, and I'm thinking I'm no Sam Donaldson, he's not going to tell me anything anyway, so I'm not going to ask anything about the latest situation. Then Clinton leans over to me and Pena, and not prompted, said there's nothing to this Monica stuff, nothing at all; there's no more to this than us blowing up TWA Flight 800.

He made the comment, and Pena and I said OK. Then we go out and I gave Clinton a good introduction and a fair one. Said how I had known him. Said he had always been fair to mayors. Each year, Clinton had made himself and his Cabinet personally available to mayors, not like it was before. It's a privilege to come to the White House but it also shows the respect he had for mayors throughout the country. And it said a lot about him.

Also, on issues of concern to cities, the response usually was positive, whether about fighting crime or reducing federal mandates. The final point, I had known him since law school and I said I believed his heart was in the right place. What I tried to say was that Clinton was trying to do well. I might not agree with how he did it. I wasn't talking about his sexual mores or anything like it. This was somebody, based on my sense of him, that I believed wanted to do good things.

## A somewhat generous introduction

Coming at the time it did, maybe it was more generous an introduction than necessary. But, I believed it. You don't stick a knife into somebody or abandon them when times are bad. Now, I got quoted in The Washington Post, got quoted in the national media, and it played back home. Obviously, just standing up there with him, getting my picture next to him when all this was breaking loose and with the controversy, brought attention to me. It made life certainly interesting.

I caught a lot of flak for it. One of the questions at the Press Club in Indianapolis with John Price, Peter Rusthoven and myself during the GOP Senate primary was about how would we introduce the president if given the opportunity. Price said he'd refuse. Rusthoven would say this is the president and sit down. And I said I already had this situation, and the first two approaches were an insult. My job as president of the U.S. Conference of Mayors was to give the presentation fairly and honestly. This shows how national politics intersect with state and local politics.

## Lied to me

It got tricky after the primary election for Senate. When the Clinton story unfolded and he gave his deposition that summer, followed by his disastrous evening statement about how he had an inappropriate relationship with Monica Lewinsky—although I suspected it all along—what really bothered me was Clinton had lied to me directly.

It's not about me. He had lied to his family, his Cabinet and the American people. But it bothered me, in that one situation; it was a gratuitous lie. I hadn't asked him about it. Pena hadn't asked him about it. He could have easily said nothing or spoken about something else.

Obviously, he was going through a stage where he was telling a lot of people lies, whether it was trying to convince others or himself he hadn't done anything wrong. I was one of the people who heard him directly saying a lie. And it hurt me. That bothered me. I know people do things they shouldn't be doing and tell lies. But you don't like being told a gratuitous lie directly.

But people aren't perfect, either.

## Cast of characters:

**Rex Early**—Former state GOP chairman; unsuccessful candidate for Indiana governor

**Charles "Bud" Meeks**—Now a state senator, he's a former Allen County sheriff who ran unsuccessfully against Win Moses in 1983

**Dick Lugar, Bill Hudnut and Steve Goldsmith**—Former Republican mayors of Indianapolis

**Bruce Babbitt**—Interior Secretary under Clinton

**Frederico Pena**—Secretary of Energy under Clinton

# I FOUGHT THE CITY COUNCIL AND WE BOTH WON

*Photo by Staff photographer*

**Swearing in**

City Clerk Sandra Kennedy swears in the City Council in 1996, the last that Paul Helmke would witness during his term. As mayor for a dozen years, Helmke had to find common ground with three sets of councils. Standing, from left: Archie Lunsey, D-1st District; Don Schmidt, R-2nd District; Tom Henry, D-3rd District; Tom Hayhurst, D-4th District; Dede Hall, R-5th District; and at-large Republicans Marty Bender, John Crawford and Rebecca

Ravine. Not pictured is the late 6th District Democratic Councilman Cletus Edmonds. Standing behind Hall is Paul Helmke's father, Walter P. Helmke.

Relations with City Council were always interesting.

It really is a challenging structure; sometimes you look at the council as the board of directors for a company, with the mayor as CEO. Other times, it clearly is a separate branch of government with its own agenda, quirks and adversary positions.

I ended up with a good relationship. When I ran in 1987, council was 8-1 Democrat; afterward, it was 7-2 Democrat. Starting out, I wasn't sure what the relationship was going to be. Because of the partisan split, and because they'd all been there so long with a lot of experience, I clearly was the new kid on the block from a different party who had beaten somebody—Win Moses Jr.—they had supported and worked with.

It made things tense and tricky. I came to the council meeting the first time after being elected to extend an offer of conciliation. I wanted to work with them. They were all different types of personalities.

**Schisms and rifts**

Part of what helped me early on was the fact Democrats had such domination for so long they had developed their own schisms and rifts within the dynamic of council. For example, Mark GiaQuinta would argue with Janet Bradbury; others would argue with each other. Council developed into two or three groups. Don Schmidt and David Long as the two Republicans; Tom Henry who would try to work with Schmidt and develop coalitions with others; Paul "Mike" Burns, the former mayor, always taking his own iconoclastic position; Jimmy Stier, along with GiaQuinta, taking the strong Democratic Party line on issues.

GiaQuinta saw himself as the person who had to take up the flag as the leader of the deposed Moses administration, and Stier was his ally.

It was a group that had a lot of reasons not to like me, but it also had a lot of reasons not to like each other. So putting together a coalition with these shifting groups turned out to be a challenge.

Also, I had to establish my credibility and that of my administration. A big plus was having David Silletto as controller; he was well-known and respected in the community. A bit older, he had some of that gravitas and sense of wisdom. Through some marriages, he was related to the GiaQuintas. It helped develop some personal connections. It helped, since an early focus with council was on financial issues. If I was talking numbers, I was attacked as not knowing what I was talking about. It was sort of the spin Moses put on occasionally when he'd speak out about city finances.

It was like fighting the 1987 election all over again, dealing with similar issues a year later. One of the most amazing stories was how the Democrats had a retreat early on after I took office and brought in a facilitator to help them all get along better. I'm not sure how successful it turned out.

But I didn't want to approach issues with a partisan attitude, especially with seven Democrats against you. I needed to do a good job for the city, and to break down the sense Democrats should be against me because I was a Republican who had beaten Moses.

The fact council members were there for a while probably helped me; they were independent and had their own priorities. Stier, for example, might be Mr. Democrat and out to get me on every level on the partisan side.

But he also was Mr. Neighborhood, and anything we were doing to strengthen neighborhoods and public safety would help him be our ally.

With each we could find something we could work with.

## Alliances

I would try to meet with each of them separately; each was different. For some, Silletto would be better working them; for others, my chief planner John Stafford. We tried to do it on an individual basis; each had their individual quirks.

I remember Burns meeting me early on and getting his perspective. It was interesting. Here was somebody who had run in every election since 1947, either for the council or mayor, and he gave me some of his insights from how things were when he was mayor. Things had changed but he was still helpful. One of his suggestions was to see a copy of everything that went out from every department. Maybe it was easier in the 1960s when you didn't have copy machines and things weren't as big. But the basic point was to keep your eye on the little stuff, and the advice was good. Those little details could end up biting you. I wanted my folks to be able to have the same attitude, to look carefully at the details.

It was battle stages the first 18 months, until we had gotten through two income tax votes and started the St. Joe Township annexation. And council members were quick to let me know when they weren't going to give in on things that I had wanted. In mid-1988, I wanted deputy mayors and they shot it down before the notion had gotten very far. Council perceived it as a threat to its position; they didn't want anybody other than the mayor with a title of mayor. They could accept a chief of staff, but not the concept of a deputy mayor.

## Workings

I believed I learned a lot about how council worked, and so did my staff. We ended up working better together. We developed a different way of working with council. When Moses was there, for example, budgets were pretty much decided behind closed-door settings largely because he was a Democrat with a Democratic council majority. Democrats would support Win; Republicans would be ignored in the equation and most issues were settled before they became public.

By the time I came in, the biggest challenge was to get it out of a confrontational mode of Republican vs. Democrat. It took us about 18 months, but we established ourselves as people who wouldn't pull the wool over their eyes. Police Chief Neil Moore and Dave Silletto had a lot of credibility with the council. By the time of the second income tax vote, it was the start of a new era in my administration's relationship with council. It switched from an adversary role to "what can we do" with income tax money to help neighborhoods in the six council districts.

The council even sat in on budget discussions, and it helped make the relationship less adversary. While over time the political mix changed, from Democrat majority to Republican, my relations with council remained very good.

## A good setup

We've got a pretty good setup here. I would talk with other mayors in the country who couldn't get anything done because of their relationship with their councils. The best thing we got going here is the strong mayor system of government, where people elect the mayor and the mayor has some power. He's seen as the person in charge. When things go well, he gets the credit; when things go poorly, he gets blamed.

The mayor here has enough power to effect change and take care of any problems that develop. In cities with city managers, a council selects the manager. He does most of the hiring and runs the operation, and theoretically, he doesn't set policy but carries out policy from the mayor. But it's so hard to separate policy from implementation because the way you do things sometimes defines what the policy is.

Most people here don't appreciate how well the system works. For example, when the mayor sends down the budget, the council can subtract from it, but not add to it. As a result, there's no line-item veto; if the mayor doesn't want it, he doesn't put it in the budget. Council members can't add it. If the mayor decides not to spend it, the council can't either. That's not the way it is on the federal level.

Council also has a lot of power it doesn't use. Often, its greatest power wasn't from ordinances that were introduced but comments they would make. It would define an agenda for government. It's the same when conducting hearings on issues, like with the police chief to address the crime rate.

While checks and balances are great, as chief executive I'd get frustrated at times with council. So we figured out ways to perhaps get things through easier. And the council often would help by not asking the appropriate questions, even though we had the answers.

If there were controversial items in the budget—and those were hard to hide—I wanted arguments to be over major ones, not hour-long arguments over pennies, like should this person get a new car or should there be a new desk for somebody. You have to watch every penny, but in a $100 million-plus budget, the extra $2,000 here or there—while it adds up—wasn't worth the scrutiny if paying attention to little details meant you missed the big budgetary picture.

Council sometimes made bad decisions by eliminating things that were really needed, like a desk. We'd get to the stage where the council would approve the extra personnel but not the desks or equipment for them. It didn't make much sense. Often, it was political posturing to show they were cutting the budget by whatever percentage possible.

## Battles on our turf

Some of the things we did were calculated to make it clear battles would be fought where we wanted the battles fought. We did it in ways that were dictated by screwy state law. Normally, the salary ordinance came down a month before the budget came down. And the salary ordinance determines the job slots and what they would get paid. This would come down to council, and it didn't determine how many people would be in those job slots. And we'd have arguments with council about these job slots before we had to show them the entire budget. Sometimes, when we wanted to add somebody, we determined it by having cuts elsewhere, but until you saw them in the budget, you didn't see them in the salary ordinance to get the full impact of what we were trying to do.

Eventually, state law was changed so both the salary ordinance and budget could be looked at together. And it helped quite a bit.

One of the easiest way to sidetrack an attack, when someone's arguing, "What about such and such?" is to tell them to turn to Page 350 in the budget books we put together and that would shut them up. The more information, even if controversial, the better. What brings down mayors and administrations more than anything is trying to hide things. When you try to hide something, it's going to come out sooner or later, and then you won't have an answer and wind up embarrassed. Folks will be a lot more skeptical the next time you want something.

Complete disclosure works a lot better than playing games. It's one of the reasons why, over the years, the budget process went smoothly.

## Vetoes

When it came to vetoes, I had a few. A strong mayor has the power, but it isn't great. You need 5 of 9 on council to pass an ordinance. A mayor can then veto an ordinance, but it takes only six votes to override it. Actually, the only time a veto carries a threat is when a council vote is 5-4. Overwhelming majorities, otherwise, will overrule a mayor's veto. As a result, I didn't use a veto very often.

Also, most business sent down to council were ordinances we initiated, not those crafted by the council. If anything, it would be council-crafted ordinances we might object to that could lead to a mayoral veto. Why would I veto an ordinance I had sent down?

Council is weaker this way as well. We would send down ordinances that council didn't like. And if council didn't like it, council should have amended it. Instead, council would say it didn't like an ordinance and then send it back to the administration for rewriting. This was done often because members of council knew an amendment couldn't get five votes for passage. So it was sent back to the administration to clean up or change, and we had to figure out a way to make everybody happy.

I'd rather see council fight some of these issues in public. It's good for the system instead of having city officials doing two or three rewrites of ordinances to make council members happy.

## Smoking ban

Most of the vetoes were symbolic, often because I didn't like a position the council was taking. But not on a smoking ban in restaurants. It wasn't symbolic. It was challenging, and an ordinance that passed council by a 5-4 vote.

The smoking debate had been an issue for some time; it came from several council members. My attitude was a bit ambivalent on the issue. I hate smoking and have never smoked. I can't stand cigarette smoke. I don't like it in a restaurant, and it has an effect on where I dine. I'm very sympathetic to that side of the issue.

However, I'm always leery of government telling business what it should and shouldn't do. It's a tricky issue because it concerns public health and safety, while it also interferes with the private sector.

I was concerned whether the ban was just going to be in the city, or countywide. There's a lot of legislation on the local level that has an anti-urban bias; it only applies within city limits, not the suburbs. It puts city residents at a disadvantage, like storm water regulations that apply to homes within the city but not outside. This issue was coming down that way. I felt it should be done more broadly, countywide.

Early on, I told anti-smoking folks what I was thinking and if a ban was made countywide, I'd be inclined to go ahead with it. Early indication was council was going to go along. But, they couldn't get the county to come along. I wanted to witness a news conference, for example, with at least two of the three county commissioners and anti-smoking advocates supporting a ban. Apparently, the support from the county wasn't forthcoming. It changed the equation and I told them that. It's one of the reasons I vetoed the ordinance.

**Balancing act**

It also came down during a tricky time as I'm running for the Senate, and this was an issue that could get statewide focus. I was perceived as being not conservative and Republican enough on issues. I tried to do what's best and the chips would fall wherever with the politics of the whole thing. I ended up deciding the bill was poorly written, with too many exemptions and it wasn't countywide. It would have been an enforcement nightmare. I signed the ordinance banning smoking in businesses. At least there, the argument of competing sides tipped to a ban in the work place, because at least you have a choice where you eat, not as much where you work.

Here's a 5-4 vote in favor of a ban, so I believed my veto would be held up. I believed I had written a convincing argument in my veto against a ban on smoking in restaurants, and believed it would at least support the four who had voted against it. Instead, it drove two of the council members who had voted against the smoking ordinance to vote for it and for the veto override, giving the council six votes to carry the day. I'm still not sure of the logic. I guess Councilman Archie Lunsey was persuaded with concerns about children. With Councilman Tom Henry, I'm still not sure what went on.

It showed the limitation of a veto. Here, I believed a veto would make a difference. Instead it drove the vote the other way. It makes you wonder.

## Not smart politically

A lot of the things I did were not the smartest politically. My attitude has always been, you run for office and when in, you do the right thing. The challenge is to determine what is the right thing. There are legitimate disagreements about what is the right thing. It has to be best for the folks as a whole, and you don't let it affect aspirations about running for office in the future. On every issue, I tried to do what I believed was the right thing. At the same time, I was aware of the political ramifications of my decisions.

With smoking, it was more why does this issue have to come up now? Why not earlier or later? But council was driving it, and that's when it was decided.

The annexation issue, overall, has hurt me politically over the years. In terms of running for future office, one of the local GOP's strengths are the Republican suburbs around Fort Wayne. Annexations have not made me popular in those areas. It's something I've heard being talked about statewide, and it slopped over into the Senate race and elsewhere.

While I'd spoken about the issue in the past, what fooled people was their belief, "He's talking about annexation, but he's really not going to push it." Or, "Even if he's going to push it, it's not going to happen." Politicians throw around issues but often either don't believe in them or don't try hard enough. Even when they do, there are so many built-in barriers to major change it isn't going to happen here.

What fooled people here is I not only talked about annexation, I did it. And I continued to push it aggressively. People aren't used to it from politicians, especially politicians realize there's political cost. It played a role in my popularity, in the Jill Long-Dan Heath campaign for U.S. Congress, and the Linda Buskirk-Graham Richard mayoral election. It also played a role in some of the support behind former Sheriff Joe Squadrito, not only in the GOP primary election he lost to Buskirk, but in disputes over the years.

The income tax and tax reform measures also keep getting thrown back at me. The winner in the Senate race, Evan Bayh, had print media attacks on taxes; the GOP's Peter Rusthoven and others mentioned it in the Republican Senate primary race. Any politician with a connection to a tax hike, even if it's balanced with a tax cut, is going to have danger. Folks will dig out the tax hike but not mention what it paid for, like police, or that it was balanced out the next year with a tax cut. It's almost radioactive in recent years politically to have any connection with a tax hike. It means people get afraid to make any changes, even if cutting one person's taxes means raising another's.

It didn't hurt me so much in local elections; the issue of the income tax here is not controversial. But it's sitting there in the files and I'm sure if I ever decide to run again for public office, someone's going to dig out "Helmke's had 12 tax increases."

But they won't remember all the tax decreases that balanced them out.

## Cast of characters:

**Mark GiaQuinta**—A 5th District Democratic City Councilman, he served four terms before stepping down in 1995; a local attorney

**David Silletto**—Former Lincoln National Corp. executive, Silletto served as Helmke's controller, responsible for city finances

# I'M THE TAX MAN

The entire financial issue came up in my first campaign.

It was sort of strange. It wasn't somebody taking money from city coffers, or misusing city property, as has been the issue with some past administrations.

Instead, it was a concern in general with the way the city was handling its finances. Some economic development projects went bad, like Micro Standard, where $1 million was given out to a fledgling company and never repaid. The public had some sense of these problems and how they tied in with other concerns about how honest and straightforward was Win Moses Jr. And it all tied in with the campaign finance reporting fraud allegations Moses was charged with, and eventually plead guilty to, that maybe the city's finances weren't being taken care of as they should.

The economic times of the mid-1980s were tough. As a result, the city was doing things a bit more creatively to attract industry and jobs. Where Win was trumpeting his creative financing, people started to look at it as smoke and mirrors. There was a big question mark hanging over the city's finances when I came into office.

**What shape were we in?**

So, what kind of shape were we really in financially? I wanted to be very careful and not lock myself into a "no new taxes" pledge. I wanted to keep open my options until I looked at the books. The new controller, David Silletto, and John Stafford, my chief planner, started to look at the situation and found ourselves with concerns. The city's cash balance at end of 1987 for day-to-day operations was $84,000.

I remember one meeting where we talked about our financial shape, and it struck us as not a lot of money. Obviously, as an individual, I'd love to have $84,000 in the bank. But Silletto noted $84,000 was enough to run the city until 3 p.m. on Day One. And that's it. It's not a very healthy cash balance.

Meanwhile, the utilities were not in good shape; they had a pooled cash arrangement. A lot of the cash for the water and sewer utilities was pooled so it looked like you had enough when you had to buy something. But, in effect, you kept borrowing from the same pot and shifted around the money. Thus, the utilities were pretty much in the red; the civil city side is pretty much out of money as well. Our bonded indebtedness showed a lot of them had balloon payments at the end coming due within that year or next. There was a backlog in projects and petitions from homeowners to the Board of Works for neighborhood improvements.

The first hint of bad news came up during the election when Moses proposed a budget for 1988 that contained a 3 percent property tax hike. Earlier in his second term, Win made a big deal about not raising taxes. And then when the city raised taxes by 3 percent in an election year no less, it struck me as a sign of danger.

We needed to respond quickly and put together our fiscal recovery plan. We dealt with the issue of a local income tax. We looked at cost-cutting, like self-insurance and doing away with take-home cars for department heads and other top officials. Those were supposed to save close to $1 million.

We adopted a position of no salary hikes for the next year, and some utility rate hikes to take care of that side. The biggest one, however, was the income tax.

## Income tax

A local income tax never seemed to be much of an issue during the campaign. I believed it wasn't something we needed at the time.

But when I got in, Allen County was pushing for the County Option Income Tax to help its financial situation. When I found out our situation, I got behind COIT right away. The tax had to be adopted by end of March 1988; it was a tight timetable. The City Council was the deciding group over COIT.

County officials came before the City Council at a public hearing to push for COIT because the county was spending a lot on the criminal justice system.

Supporters also noted what this tax could do for other units of government. Our arguments focused on the city's needs as well; we lobbied for it.

However, Moses was in town and got the Democratic-controlled City Council against it; he was posturing a bit. When Moses was mayor, he said there would only be an income tax over his dead body, even though I don't remember the income tax being such a big issue when he was mayor.

But his opposition argument to the council made it tough for tax supporters. I recalled Win saying with him being out of office and unemployed, the tax would become burdensome. But Win had some healthy income and assets from his business interests so I'm not so sure about that argument.

And it struck me Win had it backward. If he were truly unemployed, having an income tax would be better. If property taxes had to go up, it would raise the taxes on his nice home on Westover Road. But if we had an income tax, and he was truly unemployed with no income, he wouldn't be paying anything extra.

## Politics and posturing

It was more the politics and posturing of the matter that scored points. Headlines at the time were more about Win fighting back against Helmke. Some of the charges he made were we didn't understand finances and how things worked. It came down to City Council; we ended up losing 7-2. But it was a vote we felt we had a chance to carry. Once you lost one person, you lost others pretty quickly. One of the crucial ones was David Long, and I remember speaking with him once at the office about the tax right before the vote. And David had to walk around the block afterward to think about it. We ended up not getting his vote.

Our hopes to get others were lost, and we couldn't get the five votes necessary to pass it. It went down and that was very disappointing. It meant we had to try harder with other cost-cutting moves.

Looking back, we made such a big deal of cutting $1 million that first year. Yet years later, people still said we did nothing to tighten our belts. It's the frustrating part of government; you don't get the big headlines from self-insurance, from cutting this or cutting that. Even when you do, nobody remembers a year later when the furniture's falling apart in the City-County Building and you're trying to make ends meet.

## Tax study

We started to lay the groundwork for the income tax in the future by creating a blue ribbon committee, including Mark Rosentraub from Indiana University-Purdue University Fort Wayne, for a real outsider's and expert's look at the city's and county's budgets.

The group came back in December 1988, and I was surprised by it. It said the county was in better shape than the city and the city really needed to diversify its tax base. We had heard so much about the county's problems we maybe never knew to what extent we were in trouble.

The study did some long-range projections that found assessed valuation growth that fuels property tax revenue was occurring outside the city. And it found tax abatements for economic development projects in the city meant dollars weren't going to be there for a while.

As a result, we used the study to push for COIT and why the tax made sense.

**Everybody pays**

I'm still fighting this battle today when I'm accused of raising taxes so many times as mayor. The point I was making at the time was that 60 percent of the city's income came from property taxes; the rest, from fees and other sources.

By putting the tax burden on the homeowner, we were hurting them and ourselves. We were hurting the individual because you're paying the property tax regardless of whether you have a job, and you owe the tax regardless of your cash flow. An income tax meant you wouldn't be paying it unless you had income and more only when your income went up.

For the city, an income tax was better. Everybody in the county would be sharing the tax; it helped balance inequities between city and non-city residents with better distribution based on your property tax levy. And it would allow the city to keep the property tax low in Fort Wayne.

Nobody likes taxes; they should be geared for those who benefit from government services. You get those who live here with a property tax, those who work here with an income tax, and those who shop here with a sales tax. Indiana doesn't allow local government to do a sales tax, but it could do the others.

The most crucial benefits meant all your eggs weren't in one basket; there was diversification. A property tax will stay generally flat; it'll stay just about the same whether the economy is going gangbusters or not. An income tax will go up when times are good; down when times are bad. We had hit rock bottom with the economy around 1983-1984. Now, we were on the upward swing but the city wasn't getting much of the benefit of the economic prosperity because it was reliant on the property tax. To me, the Moses administration was doing a lot to pump up the economy with economic development yet the city's coffers weren't benefiting from those extra and higher-paying jobs.

With the economy strong nearly throughout the 1990s, we've been able to benefit from the income tax. And it helped us keep the property tax low.

### COIT redux

So, when it came to COIT a second time around, we used a different strategy. We basically ignored the county, townships and other units of government who stood to get some money from COIT and concentrated on the city with a plan I was confident City Council would pass. If passed, we pledged to keep property taxes down and we ended up keeping those taxes frozen for some time.

We also phased in a local homeowner's exemption at 8 percent, which took that much off the entire property tax bill. While the rate stayed flat, for the homeowner there also was an 8 percent tax break. We put this in and we kept it there.

As I look at my personal property tax bill, and with the city about a third of my bill, my taxes have basically stayed flat over the last decade.

Also, we created a pool of funds for the six council districts for neighborhood improvements. It helped move some of the backlog of petitions for improvements in neighborhoods by setting aside a fund of money just for that use.

### 'Pork barrel' politics

Also, it was a little bit of congressional "pork barrel" politics. By having COIT money to spend on improvements, it gave district City Council members money they could take back to their constituents and say, "I've delivered. Here's the funds and we can do these projects."

It tied in with community-oriented government because it empowered people more in the decision-making process. It put more power back in the neighborhoods.

It used to be neighborhoods would come to the mayor and say we need this done, and we'll try to marshal our political clout to put pressure on you to get it done. The mayor would feel the pressure. The mayor would hurt people if they were turned down, and made them happy if the projects were approved.

With this new pool of COIT funds, the pressure was put on council members and neighborhood residents, who would petition their council member for improvements. In effect, it took some of the political heat off me while I still got credit for the projects because I was the one who had pushed COIT.

It really got the neighborhoods working together as well; no more, "I'm on my own against the rest of the city." Instead, it made neighborhoods aware although their streets might be bad, their neighbors next door might have streets even in worse shape. So we'll fix yours this year and we'll do mine next.

It was a whole different mind-set where neighborhoods had to make priorities for a limited yearly amount of money for improvements. It really started to change the mind-set of politicians and homeowners. They knew the money would be there, and working with other neighborhoods, could get something done.

It was a great package, but we still had a tough time getting COIT through, with 5-4 passage by the council. We were sweating bullets until the council passed the tax.

## Last-minute roadblocks

I still remember Jimmy Stier of the 6th District, who at nearly the last minute, asked council attorney Stan Levine to research COIT about some technicality. And the auditor was supposed to file some documents before the tax was passed. But an issue came up whether the auditor had done it, and it came up as a surprise move. I remember having to track down Auditor Linda Bloom, who had an unlisted number, and had her sign an affidavit to get on file to show the tax was being done according to procedure. But we almost lost on a technicality.

I consider the passage of the tax one of the most significant things we had ever done. While the tax remained an issue for some time, 10 years later you don't see anybody campaigning for mayor or City Council saying to get rid of the income tax or roll it back. It's something folks really accept and realize it helps the city.

## Politicking council

Part of the whole COIT vote was the issue how I dealt with City Council. This was a major piece of legislation, very public and controversial. Here, I'm a Republican with a council that's seven Democrats and two Republicans. It's obviously a difficult thing to get through. Part of what we tried to do is work with council on proposals they'd be willing to support, like neighborhood improvements.

With local issues, party lines very rarely define votes. But with Moses just out of office, it had a lot of potential for partisan vote. Part of my theory was that council was Democrat for so long, it no longer was a cohesive unit and had fallen into factions. So we weren't stuck with a two-Republican, seven-Democrat split on issues, but with two

Republicans—who sometimes didn't agree with me as well—and seven Democrats with their own shifting coalitions. We worked with Tom Henry, for example, and his coalition wasn't always the same as the Mark GiaQuinta-Jimmy Stier coalition.

For me, the challenge was to keep the two Republicans together for a crucial vote like this, and get three of the seven Democrats to go along. It worked well later on when there was less partisanship and less suspicion.

But the COIT vote still had the partisanship with it. Jimmy Stier was the good, traditional Democrat trying to keep together what Win had talked about. Tom Henry was more of an independent and somebody we worked closely with.

## Utility woes

The utilities, meanwhile, also were part of the fiscal recovery plan. We pushed for a sewer rate hike in 1988. The reality? We were in bad shape. With COIT defeated in 1988, we needed to deal with utilities directly as well to determine what was needed. Pushed for a pretty major sewer rate hike, about 25 percent.

Interesting enough, the situation pointed out how bad of a shape we were in with some of the lowest rates in the state. We were in lousy shape with our cash flow and our balance sheet. We were in a poor position to do a bond issue because we were not healthy enough financially. The poor position would have gotten us a low bond rating that would have cost ratepayers even more. The system itself was failing in places. As a result, it was easier than other areas of government to show how bad things were and what needed to be done.

It was hard to let homeowners see how bad things were; we needed to make an issue they'd believe in. It was no longer just an accounting issue; we couldn't fix the sewers unless we had more money to spend on it.

Fiscally responsible meant you had to have the revenue to cover what needed to be done.

## Stock tips

One of the reasons we used the city's longtime utility adviser, Municipal Consultants, to help with the rate increase was because its top guy, Bernard Perry, did a good job and he had a good rapport with council. As the new guy on the block, I needed to make sure council had someone else it could comfortably deal with on the rate hike issue. And Councilman Paul "Mike" Burns had a good relationship with Perry; Burns, a utility expert, was opposed to almost anything going up. So we believed if Perry could persuade him, we could get things through.

It didn't hurt that Burns always wanted stock tips from Perry, especially after meeting with him on utility matters.

Burns was against the income tax because his property taxes were very low. He had a small house and lived frugally. With his investment income, however, he did very well, so COIT affected him a lot more.

But as a former mayor, Burns knew what the utility needed to stay viable.

## The politics of rate hikes

There had been a few rate hikes, normally single-digit, in the past. Past politics dictated rate hikes not exceed single-digit because it would look bad with voters.

We went in the first year and said we can't play these games anymore because we wind up with things falling apart. If we don't bite the bullet and pass an increase that works, the situation won't improve. I wanted the consultant to tell me what was needed, and I was willing to follow the number even if it wasn't popular politically.

About the only time I intervened was when, for example, you were at a suggested 30.1 percent rate hike and I would push for a 29.9 percent amount. It's the old marketing tool: always choose the lower number.

However, I believed the general public really didn't differentiate much or give you as much political heat if it was a 37 percent rate hike vs. a 31 percent increase.

Instead, the instructions were to do what was needed to get things right, and I'd pay the political heat to push them through.

So, here's the push for income taxes, higher utility rates, a property tax hike for 1989, and people were saying it was politically controversial. It was a time George Bush was running for president and saying "Read my lips." Evan Bayh was running for Indiana governor on talk of "no new taxes."

## Do the right thing

I remember folks coming to me and saying, "Helmke, what's wrong with you? You have a GOP president saying read my lips, a Democratic governor not raising taxes, and you're raising taxes and utility rates."

My response was you do the right thing. Politically, it would be great not to have to raise taxes but we were in such bad shape, the situation was really perilous for the city and things needed to be done.

## The politics of taxes

The income tax reared its head politically in 1989 during the special election for Congress.

One of my political strategies was if you have tough things to do, like adopt a new tax, do them early. There would be some pain, but you'd see benefits shortly thereafter. And by the next election in 1991, people would see roads getting fixed and utilities in good shape because of the extra tax revenue.

However, we had a special election in early 1989, and it threw a lot off that strategy. Sen. Dan Quayle was chosen vice president, Rep. Dan Coats takes over as senator, and there's an open congressional seat, with all this happening at the end of 1988. This is right at the time I'm getting the report on the condition of the city's and county's finances and am pushing for a utility rate hike.

It affected me several ways: I had to determine if I wanted to run for Congress. I had run once in 1980, and it's something that sounded interesting. But I had just been elected mayor and had been in office less than a year. Voters didn't like politicians who shift gears and keep running for something else.

Also, I believed the income tax was a hot issue, along with the St. Joseph Township annexation, and if I ran for Congress, those issues would become politicized, at least on the City Council level. The tax would not be passed by a Democratic City Council. No way was the council going to approve major initiatives from a Republican congressional candidate.

So I decided not to run. But Dan Heath, my safety director at the time, decided to run. He was closely aligned with me; Heath used some political muscle to get himself nominated by the GOP caucus. Folks thought it couldn't be done; that I was weak because of these controversies and thus Heath would be a weak candidate for Congress as well. But getting him a victory from the caucus showed I had political clout.

Then, during the special election against Democrat Jill Long, she hammered Heath on the income tax and on annexation. Those weren't issues relevant to the congressional race, but that's politics.

### Pretend you don't know Helmke

Heath was getting advice from the national GOP campaign people. The message was: You don't know who Paul Helmke is and don't have anything to do with him.

Heath had been a part of my campaign and my administration, and really I believed he had gotten the nod from the Republicans because of what we've done. I don't mind taking political heat if someone can win, but I believed it was bad campaign advice from the national folks.

The way to respond about tax grabbing, for example, was to blame it on the sad financial situation we had inherited from the Democrat Moses. The simple way was to blame it on Win.

If it's horrible Helmke is raising sewer rates and starting an income tax, my response was to say the situation financially was horrible, and the Republicans had to come in and clean up the Democrats' mess. Instead, the national advisers said to Heath, "Pretend you don't know who Helmke is and keep him in the background." Instead, they told Heath to run on the Dan Coats-Dan Heath connection from his ties working with Coats.

The advisers believed their strategy was going to win, and it didn't. By politicizing these issues in the national election, it made them more radioactive than they would have been otherwise. They took on a taint of partisan politics for years. If there hadn't been the special election or had it been handled differently, maybe I wouldn't have had the continued flak over taxes and annexation.

### No dumb politician

I'm not a dumb politician; I know nobody wants a reputation as someone who raises taxes. I had to explain what I was doing in the context of the future of the community. Most of these speeches defending myself wound up being said before Republicans. Just because Republicans believed in smaller government, and as a result, less taxes, it didn't mean sewer and water lines didn't need fixing. You still need to do these things on the local level.

Instead, a lot of people generalized "Republican" just stood for fewer taxes. I tried to argue Republicans stood for trying to solve problems on a local level, not always from Indianapolis or Washington.

On the local level, if I said you needed a tax hike for more police, next year you'd see more police. It's a difference from the state or federal level where you pay taxes in hope some of the money trickles down for local police.

It was one of the toughest things for me to deal with in 12 years. It goes back to 1987; I was seen as a good strong Republican. People wanted Win out and I was seen as a good candidate. But when the tax and annexation issues came up, there was the perception Helmke doesn't fit what we want. I've had to continuously argue what Republicanism means. If we argue we want a smaller federal and state government, and power back at the local level, the local level has to have the tools to deal with the problems. And sometimes it means having to raise taxes or utility rates.

### Republicanism

And Republicanism means you want fiscal responsibility. Smoke and mirrors, deficit spending, back-ended bonding—those sorts of things and gamesmanship Republicans don't like. It's the concept of the balanced budget, not just cutting, but getting it into balance. Some of it's through cutting; some of it could be by raising rates.

So, if you've got needs that need to be taken care of, you take care of them as much as possible with current dollars. You make the bonds as short as possible when it comes to borrowing. It means doing things the right way. But when I got criticized for doing things the right way, either by raising taxes or supporting a new income tax or higher utility rates, I had to argue for my version of Republicanism.

As a result, we set up an income tax at 0.2 percent of the adjusted gross income of every wage earner in Allen County, with 0.1 percent yearly increases, to make it easier on taxpayers and to avoid sticker shock. The bad thing about how the tax was set up is that one tax decision helped paint me as a continuous tax-raiser with five tax hikes for each incremental increase. With the county option income tax set up to go all the way to 0.6 percent, it became "Helmke raised taxes five times." It's hard to respond; I could have easily have said let's start it at 0.6 percent, and then it would have been one tax hike. But it would have taken more money from your pocket.

Incrementally is fairer to the taxpayer, but it ends up being five hikes instead of one. We could have almost argued that I could have gotten away with no new income tax, but left unchanged for 11 years a higher property tax rate and the city could have gotten even more revenue. Instead, we lowered the property tax rate in exchange for the income tax.

**Local tax reform**

By leaving property taxes at a higher level, it would have been more of a burden on the property owner, tougher on economic development, and a burden on the senior citizen. We did a tax reform package. It wasn't just getting more dollars, but moving the system from property taxes to a reliance on several sources of revenue.

I got no credit for the fact the property tax rate was 13 percent lower when I left office than when I started. Also, we instituted the homestead exemption which lowered homeowners' tax bills even more. But to my political opponents, I still had 3 or 4 property tax hikes in a dozen years.

Why? Because one year we lowered it to a 30-year low based on state estimates and those numbers proved not accurate. So the next year, we had to go back to where we were before. As a result, over the two-year period, we ended up at the same spot. In one year, there was a big tax cut nobody remembers. Instead, they said afterward, there's another Helmke tax hike. Yet all it did was bring back the rate to where it had been before. But it's all part of the political games people play.

## CEDIT and COIT

With COIT, and then the county economic development income tax, we took both up to a total of 1 percent. We moved from COIT to CEDIT because it gave the city more dollars based on the distribution formulas of COIT. For every dollar collected under COIT, the city was maybe getting 40 percent. With CEDIT, the money was distributed to other local units of government differently, and we were getting 60 percent from every dollar. If I'm going to be blamed for every $1 coming from your pocket, and I'll be blamed whether it's called COIT or CEDIT, I'll take the 60 cents for the city instead of the 40 cents.

The city also got penalized for lowering property taxes. What hurt us is by lowering our levy—the amount of revenue a unit of government can generate through property taxes—we got a smaller percentage of the COIT distribution, while other units of government, like the county at their levy limit, weren't penalized. If I hadn't put myself on the line and taken the political heat, the county wouldn't have gotten any of this new income tax revenue.

COIT, as a result, was capped at 0.6 percent; the rest, or 0.4 percent, was CEDIT.

If we hadn't had the income tax, property taxes would have gone up or services would have diminished. There was money, $450,000, in each district for improvements for neighborhoods. COIT and CEDIT were here to stay and they've been good for the community.

## Sewer and water rate hikes

Sewer and water rate hikes also were more of the same controversies—two or three hikes each for water and sewer in my 12 years. I tried one each in each term.

On the water side, the gorgeous limestone filtration plant was beginning to show its age. The laboratory was something out of the 1940s. A lot of fixing was needed. There was a lot of deferred maintenance.

We pushed through a rate hike in the 30 percent range. So in my first re-election campaign against Charlie Belch, Belch was making some noise about how we were putting in stained glass, spiral staircases and a wet bar at the plant. Instead, we were putting in glass that was for safety purposes. And in the lab, you put in faucets and stainless steel sinks because that's what a chemistry laboratory needs. But for politics, we were putting in stained glass and a wet bar. We had to point out to people that's not what we were doing.

The danger in public life, if you make tough decisions, you'll be attacked from every angle. It comes from Republicans for raising rates; the same with Democrats, the media and the public. You need to spend a lot of time laying the case for the need for such improvements.

Politicians attacked me. But when I walked neighborhoods every Wednesday night the first six years, a good exercise that kept me in shape, only once did somebody attack me on taxes. One person in six years raised it as an issue. And that's amazing.

## People want improvements

It's not to say other people didn't care about it, but those issues are not what they complained about when they had me on their front porch. Of course, if you ask in a poll, do you want taxes to go up, the answer almost always would be no. But when you talk to people, they said we need more police, better streets, and that the sewers were backing up. Usually, they said there were needs we hoped the city would address. At some level, it's easy being mayor: I told them if you want something, you are going to have to pay for it. If you don't want to pay more, than you're not going to get it.

People would tell me there were things they wanted and those things were more important than the amount of taxes they were paying without the improvements. On the local level, you see a lot more clearly how your dollars are being spent. And most people accepted the increases. Every time I ran, the numbers went up. Folks accepted the improvements even if it meant paying more.

### Looking underground

If your water and sewer utilities aren't in good shape, you often aren't going to see a problem. It's why we made a big deal early on about the condition of the Three Rivers Filtration Plant; we could get the cameras inside to show it was falling apart. But you can't get cameras to film the problems underground, at least not very well.

We tried different ways to get people to see what we were dealing with and to show there was a need. There were a few things we did; one of the most valuable ones weren't planned.

One, we used our Geographic Information System, a computerized mapping system, to show where water and sewer main breaks were occurring. The mapping system helps makes the case by showing graphically where problems are occurring.

The first time we had it done, I assumed the older the line—and some were over 100 years old—the more likely they'd break. But the lines that were breaking the most often were those from the mid-1950s/early 1960s. One of the theories was that Paul "Mike" Burns was mayor at the time and he was known for being parsimonious. But I don't think that was the case.

Instead, it was the kind of pipe being used which wasn't as good as the older material that had been used in lines before.

## Lillian Avenue

The most obvious problem occurred in 1995 when Lillian Avenue residents started to get a lot of backup in basements. We had started looking at the combined sewer overflow issue some time before then, and had known it was a problem. The federal government was telling us about environmental concerns. The economic development folks kept telling us it's a problem as well. We had red and green zones for development based on an area's sewer capacity and condition. This showed how development could be affected because areas had a system that couldn't accommodate new construction. The Georgetown area, Southwest and around the airport, for example, these were red areas that couldn't take on another car wash or another business.

But the clearest problem area was on Lillian Avenue. We actually had dealt with the issue in 1991 when we created a sewer fee to help pay for storm water runoff. Whenever we had a big flood, the focus would be on the rivers where folks hoisting sandbags got the publicity. But there also were flooded streets that didn't get focused on because of the rivers. Heavy rains causing street backups were the next problem to deal with after river flooding.

Lillian homeowners were angry. I spoke with utility officials, and they said it's a 500-year rain that had caused those flooded basements. These are crazy numbers they use. It makes you think this is going to happen every 500 years but it actually means something else. It's more of the percent type of thing. So we get this one kind of rain, and we get some attention there.

So we tell folks it's a 500-year rain, and two weeks later, the same thing happens. It rains hard and all these basements get flooded. Now, folks are really angry; it's July 1995, an election year, not a good time for cameras getting shots of crap floating in people's basements. We can't give them the same explanation again; we have to do something.

I go out again, and walk the Lillian Avenue area. It's probably the angriest group of people I ever walked with. They were upset and had every reason to be upset. The water receded but these basements still stunk and you could see the cause. Our attitude was to use this to advance what we knew needed to be done but had never been able to get over the edge with a strong commitment from politicians and the community.

### Sewer task force

So we created the sewer task force. We got folks from affected neighborhoods, not only Lillian Avenue, but South Wayne and other not-so-obvious areas because one-third of the community is on combined sewers. We addressed the environmental and economic development components of this problem as well.

I basically said, "We'll give you all the staff and background. You tell me what you want done." The initial reaction was very suspicious. People believe it would be just another committee that would sweep the issue under the rug to get me through the election. But I indicated I'm serious; I said we need this problem addressed.

Folks worked on it close to a year. They came up with recommendations, not exactly what the utility officials would have come up with. But they were reasonable, calling for a higher level of service. I asked them how do you want to pay for it? And they said with a sewer rate close to 40 percent.

It still amazes me. I've told this to other mayors. In effect, I had this group of homeowners who were coming up to my office, shaking their finger at me, saying "Mayor you better raise these rates 40 percent or we're going to have your head. We'll protest in front of City Council and you better do this."

Usually, people approach an issue like this by being angry if you raise rates. This time, people were getting angry if we didn't.

## You want something, pay for it

To me, it really gets back to my original point: If you want something, you have to pay for it. These folks knew there weren't any options out there short of getting the sewers fixed, and they were willing to take matters in their own hands. I surprised them by saying I accept your plan and will recommend it to the City Council. And we're doing this right around the time I'm considering running for U.S. Senate.

I didn't take much local political heat for it because citizens were pushing for it. This has to be done, they said. There would be no angry citizens as long as we did it. If anything, the issue was whether politicians had the guts to go along.

It really transformed the way the debate occurred. It was citizens setting priorities, in control and pushing them through. Government's role was to be the contractor. This group even wanted to stay around afterward to make sure the work was got done.

Part of the long-range sewer plan calls for periodic rate hikes as the work progresses throughout parts of the city. It will be interesting to see if the political will continues with the new mayor and council to see this through. My sense is they will go along.

## Taxes too high?

Are taxes too high? How do you measure these things? We still have one of the lowest property tax rates in the state. The 1 percent income tax is a tool just about every other community has on the local level. And we are taking care of things other communities aren't; for example, we have an extensive curbside-recycling program.

The garbage fee was a way to address the issue, and the city made sure there was a fee for users instead of property taxes to pay for it. Costs for garbage pickup would be set by how much trash folks set out. And we still have a lower garbage rate than folks with private trash pickup have in the suburbs, and it's with curbside recycling.

My bottom line response to all this? Maybe some things have gone up, but they haven't gone up as much as the cost of inflation and other goods. We're low compared to other cities.

### How we deal with things

But the crucial issue isn't just how low we are, but how we're dealing with issues. We have good bond ratings, we're taking care of out utilities, our public works and and our Police Department. What do you want out of government? If you want it, you have to pay for it, and now people are paying for it directly. When I left office, the amount of bonded indebtedness was less than when I had taken office, yet the city was larger populationwise 12 years later.

There are so many games you can play with finances folks just don't catch on to. There's the credit card scam, basically; you could put it on your credit card. Then you can trumpet "I didn't raise any rates and I'm fixing you're streets." But the bill is going to come in, sooner or later. We came in with old bills, took care of those and current needs, and left the city in a lot better shape than we started.

Most people aren't really that upset with what we've done with finances. They'd rather have the take-home police cars, neighborhood improvements and sewer issues dealt with.

### Spin

Politically, it's tough. Again, if you want something, you have to pay for it. And if you don't, tell me what you'd like cut. I don't mind cutting back, but folks would rather pay for it than have a smaller police department, or less road improvements. That's the bottom line.

A lot of this is spin. A lot of it is headlines and puffery. When I make the point during speeches about how the property tax is lower than when I started, and I get the response, "It can't be true. My bill has gone up."

A lot of people don't know what they pay in taxes; it's other units of government that have contributed to the higher costs in many instances. How do you know if you're taxes have gone up without studying the issue? People have this instinct taxes are going up, but not knowing who's responsible. I ask people which taxes are going up the most; most people don't know. Most people, if they live in the city, believe most property taxes go to the city. And they don't, not even half.

A lot of this is educating people about taxes. But a lot of it is politics. When I ran for Senate, there were fliers on how I raised taxes 12 times. It would cover all those incremental increases without taking into account the decreases.

My gut sense is what we did with budgetary items was driven by what people wanted. If anything, I still think we do things on the cheap here. I believe we should be doing even more with services. We're a low tax community. But people want more services. And we provided it without smoke and mirrors.

### The Steve Goldsmith game

Another game is the comparison people make: "Steve Goldsmith hasn't raised taxes. Why have you?"

Steve Goldsmith's tax rate when he was mayor of Indianapolis was a lot higher than my tax rate. It's the old game: Why is it that just because he inherited a higher tax rate than I and didn't cut it that he becomes Mr. Frugal. But I'm Mr. Tax Guy even though I have a lower tax rate than he.

It's like when you talk about tax freezes: It assumes you are at the right level to start with. For some people, it might be too high; for others, too low. If anything here, we've been on the low side.

And there's one other game: Who do you give credit to? The one who's at the right weight and stays there, or the one who's 50 pounds overweight and loses 30 pounds? One guy didn't lose a single pound, the other guy lost 30, so who's in better shape?

The whole thing's silly.

## Cast of characters:

**David Silletto**—Former Lincoln National Corp. executive who served as Helmke's controller, responsible for city finances

**David Long**—Now a state senator, he represented the 4th District on the City Council during Helmke's first two terms as mayor

**James Stier and Tom Henry** Two long-time City Council Democrats; Henry still represents the 3rd District; Stier, who died in 1999, represented the 6th District for 18 years

**Charlie Belch**—Long-time local Democratic party official who lost to Helmke for mayor in 1991

**Steve Goldsmith**—Former Republican Indianapolis mayor; lost to Frank O'Bannon for Indiana governor in 1996

# NAMING NAMES

*Photo by Gabriel R. Delobbe*

### Good times

In a dozen years as mayor, Paul Helmke worked with a number of leaders in the community, in both good times and bad. This is one of the good times, when he was affecting rakish looks with City Councilman Don Schmidt, R-2nd District, at a 1988 welcome party for the annual conference of the Indiana Association of Cities and Towns.

When it comes to leadership, I look for a mix of qualities. You want some-one who's bright and not just book smart. They need an area of expertise. And it should be somebody who knows something I can learn from.

I'm knowledgeable but I like people with different areas of knowledge as well. Leaders need to be people who not only know things, but also know what they don't know. I always get suspicious with leaders and advisers who don't see the down side. You have to be able to analyze the pluses and negatives of any decision. A leader who doesn't look at both sides is going to be blind-sided by something.

You need to be able to make decisions, which isn't as easy as you think. It's being able to fit what you know with what you don't. However, if you let the pluses and minuses bounce back and forth and overwhelm you, you'll never act at all. It will be paralysis through analysis. Sometimes decisions are made with incomplete information, without all the facts. Sometimes you wish you knew certain information, but you can't afford to wait.

You have to be willing to be criticized, to take heat and accept the fact you're going to be second-guessed a lot. Almost anything you do as mayor, someone's not going to like. Often, the person who doesn't like what you do and complains gets more attention than the people who support your decision. Even if it's right for 90 percent of the people, 10 percent will hate you for it. And those people have a higher level of intensity than those who support you.

You have to not let it get you down. You have to be willing to do what's right.

You want someone who gets others to follow them, to get inspired and to act. Leadership motivation usually is the hardest part because it relies on more than just what the leader does. It depends on the group as well. You can only lead so far on your own. You also need folks who want to follow.

Leadership is not just "stand up and give a great speech and march down the street and get things done." It's laying the early groundwork; you need to lay the groundwork so people will follow you. It means working harder and connecting with voters by listening to them.

These are leaders I admire:

**Abraham Lincoln**

A real inspiration to me. He decided what was the right thing and stuck with it, despite wars and unpopularity. He was good at making decisions, sticking with them and inspiring people.

**George Washington**

He was someone who was patient; he was losing battles, but winning the war. He realized you don't just judge immediately, but look long range.

**Franklin D. Roosevelt**

He wasn't a hero when my Republican family talked politics at the dinner table. But when I read about him, I saw someone who realized the traditional way of dealing with problems might not be the best way. He tried to figure out different ways to deal with the situation and to get a mandate to act.

It wasn't just that he tried to rid the country of the Great Depression. His leadership came from the fact people saw him doing something.

**Barry Goldwater**

He was a bit naive about the way the real world worked, but he had a clear idea of his philosophy. Sometimes philosophy has to mesh with reality, but at least he had a skepticism about the role of government.

However, I never became the kind of Republican who said all government is bad.

## Bobby Kennedy

It was the sense with Kennedy here was somebody who knew government, who knew how it could be misused. But he had a vision and idealism to push people where he wanted them to go.

I heard him speak when he ran for president in 1968.

## Martin Luther King Jr.

I met him in high school in Fort Wayne.

King realized you could lead people with speeches, and figured out ways to use the system with civil disobedience by breaking the rules while playing by the rules at the same time. He went to jail in such a way to show the rules should be changed.

## Richard Lugar

As mayor of Indianapolis, he got unigov established there. He was a model for my career; he lost for U.S. Senate before getting elected during a second try.

It's amazing how much he knows about so many different things. He has an ability to analyze foreign affairs, and agricultural and urban issues. To me he's a model of who we want in government, even if he's not flashy.

## Dan Quayle

He's interesting. The attitude that Quayle was some sort of a joke—the humorous David Letterman-Jay Leno image of him—has stuck.

I'd point out, however, it wasn't fair to him. He has a good grasp of issues and people.

It's the image problem, some of which he helped feed. Some of it is the media that puts you in a box that's hard to get out. It's unfair. If you're in the public eye with a microphone in front of you 24 hours a day, you will slip up, speak ungrammatically at times, or say things that don't sound too smart.

But Quayle had a willingness to take political risks, and keep going out there even when folks continued to knock and prejudge him.

## Ed Rousseau

I've always admired him, even though he said he was going to "kick my ass" years ago when we appeared before the Legislature to argue about the makeup of the county Board of Health. He cares about the community, and has great local political experience with the City Council, Allen County Council and County Commissioner.

He gets frustrated and shows his temper very easily. But Rousseau is an advocate of economic development and the entire community. He's got a sense that we're all in this together. He's frustrated being in a system where it's not just him, but two other commissioners as well.

## Tom Wyss

He's also frustrated and with a temper, but I can't blame him. He keeps coming back with proposed laws to lower the drunken-driving threshold, like the windup Energizer bunny. He is still pushing.

## Bud Meeks

He was a good sheriff, and his experience in Washington with the national sheriffs' association really broadened his perspective. Here's a small-town boy who winds up head of a national organization and who gets invited to testify before Congress. Yet he's kept his down-home demeanor and friendliness, the same things that made him an easy-going sheriff and individual.

## Linda Buskirk

I think so highly of her. She would have done a great job as mayor. She was better prepared to be mayor than when I had run.

She understood city government, the media, has a master's degree, is levelheaded and straightforward and did a great job running the Board of Works.

It was a real loss when she wasn't elected mayor. I hope she runs again for public office; she's the kind of person you want to see involved in government.

## Steve Shine

He's a different sort of personality. The line on Shine is he's more of the cheerleader than the organizer. But he's a great cheerleader. He's got a great media sense.

It's a strange fit with him as head of the local Republican Party. But you could tell he liked politics and liked seeing his name out front. He was pretty savvy getting his name out front.

He came to prominence when Quayle became vice president. When he wanted to run for party chairman, I didn't publicly support anyone although I was more inclined to side with Shine's opponent, Alan McMahan.

The challenge for Steve was always to make sure the reality fit in with the talk. He's great at getting attention for himself and the party. Making sure he's following through, whether it's crafting a party that's more inclusive or getting good candidates, has been more of a challenge for him.

Where I've had my run-ins with Shine was when he was put in pressure situations. Because of his role as head of a countywide party, some of the things I was doing in support of the city, like annexation, didn't sit well with non-city types. There was pressure from some Republicans locally and statewide that I wasn't being Republican enough.

On one hand, we got along well, but he'd be getting pressure and Steve's the kind of person who doesn't like internal conflict in the party. So his approach was to get those conflicts mediated, like getting us together with Sheriff Joe Squadrito.

As a lawyer, he does a lot of mediation work and he's good at it. People don't see that quality. Instead, they see the brash public side. Sometimes in politics, however, you can't bring people together and you will have conflict.

When I ran for Senate, Shine was uptight when Peter Rusthoven's people brought in Bob Dole for the annual Lincoln Day dinner. The tie-in to that was they wanted Rusthoven to introduce him. So here we are, in my hometown during a primary election in 1998 for U.S. Senate and one of my primary opponents is going up to the dais and having the prominent role of introducing Bob Dole. I wasn't very happy with it; neither were my people. Rusthoven's folks, however, said they'd have Dole cancel if it didn't happen. Shine felt in the middle of some of these things and they were hard for him to handle.

Early on in office, Shine would get called on issues and he'd call me. One issue had to do with firefighters who were dissatisfied. You can't make everybody happy; there were groups of firefighters that didn't like Chief Steve Hinton or Deputy Chief Steve Adams, or were grumbling during union contract negotiations.

I was dealing with those issues and people, but when Steve got the GOP chairmanship, he'd call me about some of those gripes. I tried to be pretty direct with Steve: "This is my job, not your job. And I am going to handle it my way."

I'm always willing to get more information, and I don't want to shut the door on anyone, especially the county chairman if he has thoughts and insights. But I'm going to make the call on what the city does.

I pointed out, if folks felt the way to influence me was by going through Shine, then it would open the door for Shine to hear a lot more complaints not worth his or my time.

We came to an understanding on it fairly quickly. Subsequently, he would call me to let me know what people were saying about me; it was more of the appropriate relationship for us. I felt he was a friend.

### Neil Moore

He was a great chief for the most part; he was the right person at the right time for the department. He was chosen at a time of a lot of divisiveness. He had the skills to bring the department up to a new level. He had worked on the accreditation of the department to make it more professional. With a master's degree and working on a doctorate, he brought in ideas from the outside more than others had.

Neil was responsible for community-oriented policing and knew who had tried the concept, why it worked and where it didn't. He's an academic and a hands-on police officer. He combined the way the academic and the police officer looked at things. It really helped us build up the department; he had credibility with the City Council, neighborhoods and officers to have them buy into community-oriented policing.

There were problems at the end of his tenure when I believe he wasn't as in touch with some problems, like complaints in the minority community about police officers. I don't know if he was spending too much time on his doctorate and accreditation elsewhere.

Sometimes, Neil got accused of being too willing to back up officers without realizing there were times officers needed to be disciplined. If there was a fault, it was that he sometimes couldn't judge officers as harshly as they should have been. He came up through the ranks and served with so many of them, he sometimes couldn't see when they caused problems. As a result, it was difficult to be objective.

Still, he was one of Fort Wayne's best police chiefs and one of the best in the country. We couldn't have done what we've done with the changes in the department without his involvement.

### Dan Hannaford

He was Neil's runner-up in the selection for chief. Personalitywise, Neil was a bit more outgoing and I felt he would have an easier time selling what we were trying to do. Dan was a real close second; he became the No. 2 man and the team served the department well.

It was an easy choice for me to move Hannaford up when Moore left. He was a better disciplinarian than Neil, and it's what was needed at the time. He helped restore confidence in the Police Department with the minority community; he made extra effort to work with them. Most officers realized there was a need to be tighter with discipline as well.

Hannaford also was a big advocate of using crime statistics analysis in crime-fighting. The final numbers at the end of 1999 showed the city had the lowest crime rate since 1974.

### Sharon Banks

She's one of the real jewels of the community. After my first campaign, I asked her to join the administration, but she didn't want to leave the school system when she was an assistant principal at Snider High School. I would consult her now and then even before she finally came aboard. She eventually joined as chief of staff, a real coup for me.

She knew the community really well. Her concern was always that government deal with those people government usually doesn't deal with or listen to.

She kept things running well as a No. 2 person, but also was good as an outreach person to get government and me to deal with issues we hadn't done a good job with. She formed a mayor's youth council and a deaf awareness council, so I'd hear concerns from those groups. She was always looking for new things to get into.

She was my eyes and ears to the community, especially parts I hadn't seen or been in contact with.

### John Stafford

He knows more about local government than anybody; he's a human filing cabinet. I wanted him on board from the start. As a long-time local planner, he got me excited about the concept of consolidated government back in the times of my involvement with Fort Wayne Future. It was the same with annexation. He knows everything, it seems.

He's a good person to have around, but he's very much the pessimist. When we developed our annexation plans, he believed things would flop. We'd lose in the courts, or there'd be some other downside, he said.

He could analyze issues and see long-range consequences. He put together a list of some problems we'd have to deal with the next 10 years, like trash fees, annexation, cash balances, and we used these ideas as a work plan for the future. It gave us a good road map.

Part of his personality is perfectly suited for government. He could analyze issues neutrally. But part of his personality had problems. He would worry so much. He can look haggard and this one time, he looked even worse. I asked John, "What's wrong?" He's concerned about the assessed valuation figures at a time we were readying the budget. If those figures came in low, it would throw off our numbers. He hadn't been able to sleep at night because of these assessed valuation figures. I told him I worry about those numbers but I don't lose sleep over them. "Get a life; you can't let these things wear you down."

He cared so much about what he took on, and it made it difficult for him to leave the job at the office.

He's a great guy and was a crucial person in local government.

## Tim McCaulay

He'd been a friend of mine since the mid-1970s. I knew his wife, Janet, since high school, and my wife knew Janet since grade school. He worked for my dad's law firm and became one of my closest friends when we worked there.

I didn't consider anyone else for city attorney, even though the decision was criticized. I separated my legal entanglements from the firm when I became mayor, even though Tim stayed on there.

I wanted someone I trusted, someone I had confidence in as a lawyer and whose opinion, legal or otherwise, I sought out and listened to.

He wasn't a yes person; he would tell me things I didn't want to hear and disagreed with. As a lawyer myself, I knew what I wanted from a city attorney. You have to watch how the legal issues fit with political issues and tactical concerns. You need someone who could combine the legal, political and policy advice into one. So you don't get someone who just gives you the law, but sees its political and policy implications. I had faith in Tim in those areas.

He was the one who pushed a phased-in strategy of annexation of St. Joe Township; it helped get the annexation plan passed locally. He did a great job with it all the way through. When Tim gets on a case, he's the best lawyer I've ever seen. He's a good homework type of lawyer.

He could be frustrating. He would get his own ideas about politics, mostly on non-city issues. Sometimes they'd be nastier and more biting than how I did things. He was the one, unlike others in city government, who wasn't deferential to the mayor. I'm the boss, but I wanted advice. Since I had known Tim long before I became mayor, he was the one who would tell me if I was getting off track and would get under my skin more than others.

"Don't do that; straighten up your act." That was his message at times. He gave good advice.

He also sometimes made people angry. I had to pick up after him. Sometimes, it wasn't intentionally. Other times, it was. Politically, sometimes you need the lawyer to be the tough guy, not the mayor. I'm the one who needs to get the votes and have people like me. Tim didn't need to get votes or have people like him, and sometimes he relished the role. In tough union negotiations, he liked playing hardball.

### Greg Purcell

He was a carry-over from the Win Moses Jr. administration, and was looked at suspiciously by some of the folks because he had been there before. I always sensed Greg was a professional. If you told him to do something, he'd do it. Greg would tell you if you were on the wrong track, but if you wanted it done, he'd do it.

He's a city manager type. He'll do a good job and do it professionally. In some ways, he's a consummate bureaucrat. For some people, it's not a compliment. It's knowing how to cover your rear, to make sure you could survive.

We were having some discussion about an issue, and some of my advisers were looking one way and Greg another. Greg said he knew his job was then to fall on his sword. It's one of his strengths; he was the good soldier. I appreciated it.

He made sure we did the follow through. He made sure folks did their homework, and differing options were on the table for consideration. My style at times was to put off a decision that would be messy or make some people unhappy. Purcell would make sure the issue was resolved and not left hanging. He helped drive the agenda. He knew which buttons to push and how to get government to work.

I supported him as parks director. Despite his lack of background, he's a person who learns quickly.

He can take credit for creation of Headwaters Park. When Greg came aboard as chief of staff, he said if the commitment's there, we'd get it done by 1995, the next election. He got on it, and figured out how to finance the land acquisition. If Purcell hadn't been there with his bureaucratic sense of knowing when talk is enough and action is called for, we wouldn't have Headwaters Park. Greg was the one who pushed to get it done and figured out how to get it done. You need someone who can translate visions and speeches and architectural drawings and pretty pictures, and ultimately dreams, into reality.

He also was brutally committed to his sense of ethics. One of the areas was politics. I'm getting ready for re-election in 1991 and again in 1995. I wasn't the kind of person who said people had to contribute. I'm pretty low key, but I liked to invite people to fund-raisers. Greg never sent me a single contribution to anything, and other people knew this and it bothered them. He's a chief of staff and he's not doing anything politically. But he was honest about it. He was a member of the International City Managers' Association. In such cities, city managers are non-political because it's the way the system is set up.

I told him that's fine, but here in Indiana it's a political system. I'm not telling him to contribute, but I was concerned about his credibility with the staff. If he were seen as "holier than thou" and not writing checks, it would affect his ability to do his job. He wrote the ICMA for its opinion, and the organization was pretty clear about staying non-political.

It said a lot about him. He has a high sense of standards.

Instead, he would offer to make a contribution to charity like the group that was raising money for Headwaters to show it wasn't the dollars, but the ethics. Or he'd pick up the tab for parties for the staff.

## Payne Brown

I'm really proud of him. Just seeing him grow into the job as public safety director over the years was really impressive. His mother, Helen Brown, used to show pictures of him to me because she was so proud of him.

He went on a Sister City trip with me to Plock, Poland, in 1991, and he wasn't yet working for me. I got to know him traveling in Poland; he had me listen to some of his rap music on his CD player.

He was bright, and someone who wanted to do a good job and make a difference. He was a fun person to be around. He took over after Mike McAlexander left as safety director. Despite being young, his law degree made him a great person to have on staff.

He met resistance; he looked at issues on his own and wouldn't consider how other people looked at things without skepticism. Despite being friends with police Chief Neil Moore, for example, he would question things. Sometimes the process of questioning made people angry and upset. But it's what I wanted from my advisers. Payne was willing to question things happening in the police and fire departments.

It's important to have civilian oversight over police and firefighters, and Payne did a good job with it.

He was not always good on follow-up; he needed a Greg Purcell next to him to make sure things were done. But he matured as a speaker and as someone who could handle conflict. When he first started out, he knew what he was talking about but he'd look at his shoes and mumble. I told him he couldn't do that and be effective. You have to project; he eventually developed a better preacher-and-politician speaking style.

He got criticized for a lot of things; one was for allegedly tipping off a drug dealer. The story behind it was the fact that police had suspected drug money was being run through some corporate books in the house of a suspect's parents. Payne knew the parents; they were well-respected in the community and elderly.

So he knew what police were planning to do; he was concerned police would go inside this elderly couple's home and start throwing over filing cabinets and knocking down stuff. So he called a relative of the suspect to make sure the relative is there when police arrive so they can go into the house at the same time, and the house isn't torn up and the mother left in shock.

I learned about this situation and had no problem with it. It wasn't advance warning but it became grist for a story Payne was tipping off drug dealers.

You don't want to second-guess the police, but the safety director has to keep an eye on things to prevent problems from happening. It's part of what Payne's job was, and it got him in hot water with police, with the community—especially the black community—at times.

## Barb Schoppman

I've known her since the mid-1970s with the Young Republicans. She was someone who likes politics but her main love was neighborhoods. At first, she wasn't interested in a job with the city. She joined later on as citizens advocate.

Her concern was a landlord-tenant ordinance; she worked on it, despite running into brick walls. That's why I was glad we finally passed one in the last few months of my administration.

She helped existing associations get stronger, but also helped restart dormant ones. She also worked with Neil Moore to put together the community-oriented government plan, and pushed hard to get neighborhood involvement prominently. I give her credit for getting the neighborhood side of community-oriented government organized.

### Don Schmidt

As senior City Council member who was in the minority for so long, it was tough for him to get used to having a Republican mayor and learn how to work with one. Our challenge with Don was how to get him on board. His natural inclination as a minority council member was to vote no or say no.

Don had always raised concerns with organized labor, wondering if the city was in a straitjacket with its collective bargaining rules. We also were concerned so we put together several changes to the collective bargaining ordinance. One was to get rid of the "me too" clause, where if one union got a certain percentage increase, the others should expect at least about the same.

City Attorney Tim McCaulay drew an ordinance and we knew the labor unions wouldn't like them. We wanted Don to champion the cause. We brought the proposal to the council, and looked at Don for leadership. Instead, Don looked at us and said, "I'm supposed to be leading the fight on this?" He wasn't used to being in the leadership role, and particularly not in this situation.

He always had a different look at life; it was insightful and intelligent, but often just a different perspective. I always had wished we could have gotten Don to work more closely with us.

He put together good working relationships with other council members, especially when he finally became council president.

The problem with Don, however, was the fact it was tough to get him to see the big picture. We'd send down budgets, and he'd attack minor budgetary items and miss the big issues.

Don did take activist roles on some issues, including the anti-smoking ordinance. How did it fit with Don's conservative, anti-government position? That was interesting. It was the same question with the landlord-tenant ordinance because of his ownership of rental properties. At first, he was resistant to change.

**Tom Henry:**

Even though a Democrat, Henry wound up a council member I worked with very closely. To get anything done in the beginning, I needed to work with Democrats and Tom was someone we worked closely with on annexation and a tax reform package.

He was in a different camp than Councilman Mark GiaQuinta and others. Most of the time, he could really do some good with behind the scenes give-and-take. He could deliver a couple of votes and get things done.

Also, Tom had good political sense. He had a political agenda but realized the benefits of working with the administration for the community's benefit. A fault was when he tried to do too much behind the scenes. Tom would try to put the whole deal behind the scenes and have council just vote on the issue in public without much discussion.

I believed there were times when the fight should have been out in the open instead of trying to patch it up privately. But he's been largely successful because of his ability to build coalitions to get things done.

## Mark GiaQuinta

He was my council member, representing my 5th District neighborhood. I knew him from the legal fraternity. He's one of the most entertaining people you could find in the political world. He was a tricky one to deal with because he's bright but you weren't sure of his agenda or where he was coming from.

Early on, GiaQuinta was the defender of the faith, of the Moses administration. He questioned closely anything I was doing. The relationship was clearly adversary for the first 11/2 years. Mark's group was different from Tom Henry's group. But Mark was tough; he knew how to ask tough questions, knowing what had been tried before. It was good for us; it kept everybody on his toes. He was a good lawyer with good cross-examining techniques, who was able to find the weak spot and exploit it.

As time went on, he got to a point where he realized we knew what we were doing. It took some time to develop.

The one hot issue, however, was the Adams Center hazardous waste landfill. It's where he tried to be more conciliatory with us, because he didn't have a lot of allies and he needed some. It was a tense issue, one of annexing the landfill despite vehement opposition from strident landfill critics. Mark and the folks at the landfill, whom his firm was representing, didn't want to get annexed by New Haven, which was fine with me. If the property's inside the city limits, we could manage the landfill's future more so than if it was on the outside.

Mark, from his perspective, was looking for any safe harbor from New Haven for the landfill. So we worked together. The interests weren't always the same, but Mark saw the advantage of working with the city.

I expected GiaQuinta or Henry would want to run for mayor against me, and in polling, threw both of their names in the hat. But it never happened.

## John Crawford

I knew him in 1987 as a contributor. He was really interested with the unigov issue at the time. When I ran in 1991, I had breakfast with him at the Window Garden and asked him for help. It's when he said he wanted to get involved in politics. I told him the GOP didn't have a full slate of at-large candidates at the time. If interested, here's an opportunity to get involved. And he did. He spent a lot of money, close to $100,000, and lost by about 100 votes.

It was interesting: When people try for politics the first time and lose, they usually say it's a stupid business and don't get involved again. With Crawford, he looked at it from his academic/medical mind-set, and analyzed what he had done wrong. He went to campaign schools and learned techniques on how to do things differently.

In 1995, he ran again, and it was a different sort of campaign. He didn't put that much of his own money into it. Instead, he had fund-raisers, in part, to show he wasn't trying to buy the election and to expand his base of popular support.

He tried some humor in his commercials. Instead of the John Crawford, M.D., in the doctor's coat, he was John Crawford looking for Elvis. The commercials came across as somewhat stupid, but at least he was trying to change the image from that of a distant doctor to more of a regular person.

This time, he won a tight election.

It's interesting watching Crawford deal with public issues. He's dispassionate. Some politicians go by gut level of what's right or wrong. His approach is cerebral. "Prove to me it is going to work or not." It's a good additional outlook for council. But he's also learned the limitations of the academic approach to politics.

It's interesting, like with Schmidt, watching Crawford's behavior on the smoking ordinance. At one level, it shows his academic analysis. As a doctor, he sees the dangers of smoking. At the same time, he trumpets himself as the fiscal conservative who believes government shouldn't be regulating things.

Maybe it's simplistic, but it shows how you bring politics in when it comes time to get elected. Then, when you're faced with the real world of actually governing, there's a role for government that might not always fit consistently with your political philosophy.

You learn really quickly in government it's not black-and-white academic discussions. It's give-and-take; where do you get the votes; what incremental steps do you take to get things done. It's probably a lot different than the medical profession, where it's clear-cut. The enemy is the disease and you fight it. In politics, it's not always so clear.

**Rebecca Ravine**

A really amazing story. Her persistence paid off in politics. She got elected in 1991 for an at-large seat at a time Republicans didn't believe the party could win a citywide council seat.

She's the council member who is willing to go out to see firsthand what's going on, like riding with police or going through training programs with firefighters. In contrast to Crawford, she has a more emotional approach to governing. It gives her some strength but some weakness as well. Her level of empathy might be great, but then the level of analysis isn't going to be the same as Crawford's.

Often, she doesn't fit into the "old boy" crowd on council and it's frustrating for her. There's a sense she gets shut out from some discussions, but nevertheless keeps on fighting hard. She's also been willing to get involved with national organizations, like the National League of Cities. My role with the U.S. Conference of Mayors was beneficial, and I was disappointed some longtime council members didn't play a role in those kinds of organizations. I encouraged Rebecca to get involved and she became a board member for the National League of Cities.

## Sandra Kennedy

I had a good working relationship with the city clerk. I've spoken with a lot of mayors over the years, and you sensed a lot of mayors and clerks were constantly fighting each other. She's someone easy to get along with. She's one of the most popular vote-getters in the city's history, even when I was winning with solid margins on the GOP side.

People liked her and responded to her. The clerk is the one person we worked through to work with council, and was vital to an important relationship. We tried to keep her informed and recognized.

She also was someone who was active with the city clerks' organization, and I was proud of her for it. Sandra's a little bit more of the old-time politician as well. She's constantly checking out the politics of an agenda.

## State Sen. David Long

I knew him from my lawyer days. We both got elected at the same time. The relationship at times was good; other times, tense. Maybe it's the nature of lawyers. We had competed in courtrooms and occasionally, we'd compete in politics, even though we were of the same political party. He gave me a lot of advice about who to hire when I got elected. Nelson Peters, for example, had been part of my campaign and he became my labor relations director.

Despite being allies, we couldn't get David on board for some of our initiatives. The most frustrating was the initial vote for the local income tax. He was really troubled by the vote. He had pressure from us to vote for what could be described as a tax hike.

Sometimes he was so torn, I felt I was dealing with Hamlet. It was hard to get him to figure out where to go.

David took issues seriously. He would brood and think and consider issues for a long time before reaching a decision. Sometimes it would frustrate us because of how hard we had to try to convince him to support us.

He was somebody who really fought for the 4th District. I remember early on, Brooklyn Avenue needed expensive repairs. We finally put together neighborhood and city funds, as well as Urban Enterprise Zone and utility funds, because of it's wide-ranging support. He was pretty dogged about getting the project done.

Also frustrating was David's ambition, then and now. There's nothing wrong with it; most politicians are. He considered running for mayor if I hadn't; then he opted to run for State Senate.

That race raised a lot of tensions. David was always supportive of our annexation efforts while on council. He never raised any serious issues and was one of our strongest supporters on annexation. But he was getting ready to run for the State Senate, and part of the area covered Aboite Township. It was presumed Mitch Harper would be running, a former state legislator, and he was raising annexation as an issue. David, in response, started to talk anti-annexation. Mitch ended up not running. But Long had already outlined it as one of his concerns.

Ron Buskirk, Linda Buskirk's husband, ran against him in the primary election and it added to the tension. Linda was one of my closest advisers and David saw that as the administration trying to take him on. Instead, it was Ron taking David on his own. I tried to stay out of primary politics while I was mayor.

He won the primary and the general election. We've had a pretty decent relationship with the Legislature, except over some of the same kinds of annexation issues. His proposals, however, were always a lot more reasonable than Bob Alderman's and others.

Actually, we laughed about how we unwittingly did Long a favor. We sent down a minor annexation before he left City Council, and it gave him his first chance to vote against it and show his anti-annexation fervor by doing so.

It bothered me he had been such a strong supporter of annexation for 71/2 years, and then when he was running for a different office, he wasn't. Part of it fits in with David. He knows how to see both sides of an issue. He was convinced, probably with our help early on, annexation was the way to go. When he was running for Senate, he heard from those who didn't like it and started to change over because of his new constituents in Aboite.

I basically stick with one position, but others sometimes change and I understand. I hope politicians don't change just because their constituencies change as well. With David, it was such a strong reversal and certainly one that bothered me.

## Bob Alderman

He and I never got along very well, particularly over the annexation issue. Bob was always one of these legislators who is fun to see, who pats you on the back and has some inside information he wants to share with you. But you're never sure where he's coming from. He's always coming up with new ideas, new jobs he's going to take. He even talked about running for mayor.

Bob was talking a lot and it was up to us to figure out when he was going to do something. When the annexation issue got hotter, Bob talked more seriously about anti-annexation legislation.

He's particularly successful with Second Amendment changes, where you haven't introduced a bill, but sit and wait while the bill gets to the floor of the House. Then, you stick your language into it.

We believed we kept things in check most of the time, but it was tough. One year, we reached a compromise with Bob for him not to try anything else in the legislative session if we wouldn't do anything further with the Aboite annexation that year. It stabilized the situation for a while.

When West Hamilton petition was filed to create a new town, however, I saw it as voiding the agreement. Bob wasn't necessarily involved with the decision, but it put the city in jeopardy.

Bob was helped out when other communities, like Elkhart and Carmel, were doing aggressive annexations; it gave him several anti-annexation allies.

The tricky part with Bob was you could never rest easy with him, because he knew the legislative process so well. If you weren't careful, something bad would wind up in legislation at the 11th hour. Bob would have his fingerprints on it, and knew what to do with legislation.

## Mark Souder

I'd known Mark since the 1960s. He's a year younger than I, and we used to go to Republican meetings for teen-agers together in high school. When I was student body president at IU in 1969-1970, he had a similar position here at IPFW. He was always a strong conservative, and further to the right on issues than I.

He was always bright, engaging and fun to argue with. In the 1970s, he used to write columns for local weeklies in the eastern part of the county. I remember clipping some at the time I was getting ready to run for Congress in 1980. I'd get into discussions with him about abortion, for example. Even though we disagreed on how to handle issues, he was some-body I got along with well.

When I ran for mayor, Congressman Dan Coats helped me with a con-tribution of about $5,000. Coats and I hadn't been close; we ran against each other for Congress in 1980. I believe it was Souder who pushed for the contribution. His point of view was Coats would be in stronger shape in Congress if there were a Republican in Fort Wayne as mayor.

He could see the big picture politically; what helped me could also help his boss at the time, Coats.

He likes politics. There are a lot of folks on the right with a conflict: They get into politics but they don't like it. They run for government but don't want government to do anything. Mark isn't for big government, but he enjoys and understands the political process. He collects political buttons, reads politics and is fascinated by it.

He's not somebody you'd pick as a successful politician. He's more of the staff-person, brains-behind-the-operation kind of guy.

He genuinely looks for ways to make life better. He looks to the faith com-munity, and recognizes government has a role it could play with the pri-vate, nonprofit sector. It's a lot better than those who say government is bad and should stay out of things all together.

## Frank O'Bannon

My father served with Frank in the State Senate back in the early 1970s. They were good friends, and my mother and Judy O'Bannon, the same. They used to go shopping for antiques together. I always heard good things about the O'Bannon family.

Despite concerns about his ties to Evan Bayh and his age, O'Bannon ran a great campaign against the much-younger Steve Goldsmith for governor in 1996. A lot of folks thought he'd be a one-term governor; but he ran again and won.

He comes across as grandfatherly; anybody who knows him, likes him. There's nothing personally to dislike about Frank. He is sincere and gracious; the criticism is, "Is he a good leader?" Sometimes issues are put off and problems occur with a do-nothing approach, similar to Bayh's. Then, when things go wrong, you don't get blamed for it because your fingerprints weren't on it.

O'Bannon's a nice person. You don't score any points by being nasty against Grandpa. It's how I've felt the times we have gotten together. It's hard to raise questions about his performance without coming across as nasty. It's the good feeling former Gov. Otis Bowen engendered.

O'Bannon was willing to make sure local issues were taken care of on the state level, especially with the 1997 tire fire on Creighton Avenue. We eventually got help from the state to clean up the mess.

### Ian Rolland

He is an example of what a community wants in a corporate leader.

I've always said—when folks have been upset with some of the things Ian has done—at least I wanted a leader who got involved on issues, even on those I don't agree with, instead of one who doesn't. The trend more and more is for leaders in the business community not to get involved. But Ian cares about this community.

Whether arts, education or downtown, Ian got involved and really helped make this place better. You are not going to see too many people like Ian anymore. He grew up in Fort Wayne, went to school here, left, and came back and became top guy at an early age at Lincoln National. He put his mark on the community. We're all better for it.

I had a run-in with him over the ballet school. Michael Tevlin, the director of the school, was a friend of mine. There were some internal arguments over direction. Ian got involved on the opposite side of me. It was frustrating; I wasn't sure how much Ian knew about the ballet school or ballet itself. Instead, I wondered if it wasn't his staff telling him this was the way to go. If he got on an issue, he had a lot of cards to play, a lot of organizational support.

He helped make things happen.

He challenged the community on airport, economic development and educational issues. It came across a decade ago as a threat when Lincoln considered, and then rejected, expensive downtown expansion. It wasn't; instead, these were legitimate issues the company had raised about the condition of the city and its educational system. But it came across as Lincoln saying it wasn't building because the airport hadn't been fixed. It gave issues attention but reinforced those people who believed things here were in horrible shape.

My biggest complaint is that Ian retired when he did; I wished he had stayed on longer. He's made it harder for his successors; his shadow affects future decision-making by Lincoln. It's tough to succeed someone like Ian who's done so well.

### Black leadership

As mayor, I watched leaders of the black community go through a period of transition. The standard leaders were going through changes. City Councilman John Nuckols had died, replaced by a slightly younger generation of Cletus Edmonds, Charles Redd, Archie Lunsey, and now, Glynn Hines; people like Payne Brown and Carl Johnson on the Fort Wayne Community Schools board; and Michael Cunegin on County Council. It was a generational transition also with the NAACP, Urban League and black churches.

When I was running for mayor, the leaders on the church side were people like James Bledsoe, Clyde Adams and Jesse White. They had been leaders for a good 30 years, and still very influential. But you started seeing a change of guard with the arrival of Ternae Jordan, Mike Nickleson and Sylvester Hunter.

I sensed there were generational tensions going on. But I dealt with all the ministers, and tried to get them all involved. Those who got involved tended to be the younger ones, especially Jordan on the park board and Nickleson on several task forces. It was important to have good relations with them, especially because of tensions between the black community and Police Department. We could disagree, but I trusted them and we remained friends.

I wanted to involve the ministerial community even more; I gave block grant money to the One Church, One Offender program, for example. It was the same with the Central City Housing Trust Fund that helped strengthen older, inner-city neighborhoods. Churches have traditionally been one of the anchors in this community. Their involvement and support was vital to any success in the central city.

### Female leaders

We've always had strong female leaders, from Helene Foellinger at The News-Sentinel, for example. But there haven't been enough women in leadership roles. I tried to promote more in city government to leadership roles, like Sharon Banks as chief of staff.

Linda Buskirk, for example, showed women could do a good job in what's considered nontraditional jobs, like head of public works.

Women have challenges men have trouble being sensitive to. Often, the male politician is used to leaving the family home and traveling, and not worrying about details. Women in politics are still seen as individuals who have to handle family responsibilities. It's not fair. A male politician can show up at a gathering by himself, stay late, and it's seen as normal. A female politician is looked at differently. It's assumed she should have an escort; she shouldn't be alone.

We need more female leaders. Nineteen of my 40 department heads were women. But we need to do more. The community is becoming a lot more accepting of women in leadership roles. We'll see a woman elected as mayor here. Buskirk helped the situation, and it will continue.

**Labor unions**

We had about nine or 10 unions, with about the same number of contracts. David Silletto, controller, worked really hard to try to get along with the Machinists Union, the largest. Because on the relatively large number of unions and contracts for each, why not a standard contract for all of them, we asked?

As I grew in the job, I realized I shouldn't complain. A lot of unions gave the mayor a stronger position. They might give you more headaches because of their number, but no one union could really stop city government in its tracks.

I've got no problems with unions or collective bargaining, but as mayor you have to make sure you are looking out for the taxpayer. In the street department, for example, we brought in outside groups to help with team-building. The unions felt comfortable enough they wound up working closely with us to make the street department and utility operations run more efficiently. That's a model of the way things should work.

There were problems. At one stage, we had a payment window in the lobby of the City-County Building. It's where people could pay their utility bills. I believe it was the bus company that wanted to see if bus passes could be sold at the windows. We figured. "Why not?" It's not too busy and we could help out customers who were there to paying bills.

The union objected, saying it wasn't in the list of their duties. That's the frustrating aspect. We weren't asking for more time or a different type of work; it was good for the community and helped another government agency. Instead, we had to go through a grievance process to get the issue resolved.

With unions, it was harder to move quickly to get changes because of collective bargaining.

It's always a challenge to make sure 1,800 city workers work as hard as they are supposed to. There were a few bad apples. Part of my standard speech for all city employees—and every month I met with all new workers during orientation, and at the graduation or the swearing-in of police and firefighters—was to remind them who was the boss. It's not just the supervisor or mayor; it's the public. It applies to all, not just elected officials.

You can't just fire someone because a TV station has videotape of the person goofing off on the job. Employees have procedures to protect them, with city policies and union contracts. There's progressive discipline with steps to take to correct bad work behavior.

In the end, there's a message not to goof off because the public is watching. When your boss is the public, you are held to a higher standard.

There were tons of people who put in tons of extra time to do good things. My overall evaluation of city workers is a good one. People really cared about what they did and put out extra effort to make things better. The public often doesn't see the extra effort and caring. I wish there were more recognition for people who did a good job.

### Intelligentsia

This town's got diffused leadership. It's changed over the years. About 25 years ago, the leadership was more readily defined. Now, it's been more weakened and spread out. The corporate climate in the community has changed; fewer of the local businesses are locally owned.

At one time, for example, you had Helene Foellinger as owner of The News-Sentinel. She, and others like her, had been around a long time, knew issues and didn't move in and out of the community very often.

After The News-Sentinel had been bought by Knight-Ridder, you had good people in charge but the situation had changed. Whether it's Peter Ridder or Scott McGehee—people who cared about the community and played a role in it—they hadn't grown up here or been in Fort Wayne all their life. Sometime, they'd move on after a few years.

They'd be members of the Chamber of Commerce, attend the meetings but got caught up a bit more in a revolving door in and out of here than in the past. Even those people who stayed longer, they became somewhat less influential.

These were sharp people, but with less of the history, and hence, less of the clout than people like them used to have.

Ian Rolland was the one exception to this, a local boy at a local head-quarters of a large company. But the last people of that kind were leaving in the 1980s and early 1990s. The ones who came afterward participated, but became less influential in decision-making than their predecessors.

The change of corporate life was obvious: These people were coming here for a few years and then leaving. I'm not knocking them, but it's reality. I belonged to this group called the Corporate Council, an organization I helped get started in the early 1980s. The idea was to get a lot of private sector CEOs together to help look at things. They took on school deseg-regation, for example. Over time, new folks replaced them and some of the replacements weren't from here. They'd be active and then be gone.

Near the end of my tenure, Corporate Council was going through a self-examination. At one of the meetings, I realized I was the only one who had been at those meetings nearly 12 years earlier. I had the longest serving tenure on this group. That says something about the corporate structure in this town.

When you have less of that stable corporate CEO structure, it makes it more of a challenge to get things done. The old model said you turned to a community made up of such people when you needed to change things. You'd get the newspaper editors, insurance and bank presidents on your side, and you could get things done.

Now, you could still get them on your side but they didn't have as much clout as in the past. As a result, it made it hard to say we're going to build this or do that.

It's one of the reasons why we went to neighborhood partnerships and their involvement with local government. The strengths of the community, the power to push change, was not going to come from above, but from below.

These were people who have a stake in their community and would push to do things. The secret was to make sure it wasn't neighborhoods vs. downtown or the corporate structure. We were able to make neighborhood groups look at the broader city interests. It was part of the magic of what we had accomplished.

# THIS IS MY LIFE!

*Photo by Helmke family*

**First day**

The Helmke family—Paul and his wife, Deborah, flanked by daughters Kathryn, left, and Laura, right—poses at the mayor's desk on the 9th floor of the City-County Building on New Year's Day 1988, Helmke's first day in office. Helmke's daughters traded places on New Year's Day 2000, his last. (See photo below.)

It's tough to carve out your own political identity when you learn about politics at the dining room table or around the living room with your father and grandfather. You get a sense of how politics works and what it can do because I grew up with it around me. A lot of the ideas and philosophy I have, as a result, are inherited.

Having inherited those ideas early, I started branching out on my own fairly quickly. There was student council at North Side High School and student government at Indiana University. How I applied those lessons often wasn't the same way my grandfather or father would have.

## At IU

When I was at IU, my father, Walter P. Helmke, was running for state Senate after being a local prosecutor for eight years. He's getting complaints from friends about these protests at the university. He didn't bother me too much; he had confidence I'd do the right thing.

But he expressed concern about the vulgarities we used in some of the slogans and chants. I don't curse very much; it's the way I grew up. I told him it's not me, but other students would use all sorts of language. We were fighting a tuition increase, and we had a bunch of posters and placards that said, "No more bullshit!" And I guess at one rally, I held this sign and he had a picture that ran in one of the student government publications that showed me holding a sign saying, "No more bullshit!" I didn't use the vulgarity, but there were these kinds of conflicts.

Mostly, my father let me make my own decisions and express my own philosophy. In the late 1960s, we argued about Vietnam and student protests, but pretty much he respected my opinions. It was the way things were after I graduated from law school at Yale and came back to Fort Wayne. We saw eye to eye on a lot of things, but not everything.

## Some advice

When I decided to run for office, my father didn't tell what to think and didn't criticize too often. He'd occasionally question what I was doing. Overall, he gave me the interest and skills in politics, and love of the political process. He taught me values, like truth and integrity and some of the Republican tenants of smaller government and fiscal responsibility, as well as respect for the law. But how I applied them was my decision.

It was great to have someone to turn to for advice, but he wasn't someone who tried to push me in one direction or another.

From an individual perspective, it was a great way to have it be. I had the love of the process and the love of politics, and the respect for what I decided without my father or grandfather telling me what to do.

## Into politics

My father wasn't surprised I was interested in politics. I was arguing it in fourth grade and showing an interest in it from early schooling. I was always wearing political buttons going back to the third grade, arguing with the teacher in the seventh grade and attending the national convention while in high school. So it was pretty clear what I was interested in. He knew I wasn't too interested in the sciences and he always encouraged me to do more with speech and debates. He'd take me to political events.

If anything, he wasn't sure if I'd be better behind the scenes or in front as a politician. As a result, his advice when I considered running for mayor was for me to support someone else and become city attorney, like my grandfather, Walter E., had done under Fort Wayne Mayor Harry Baals. Maybe my father believed it was more lucrative or personally more stable and satisfying.

## Politics are good

I've tried to encourage my two daughters to get involved in some way as well. Laura was 10, and Kathryn, 6, when I became mayor, so early on the reaction from them was a lot more negative. Unlike my father, who had a part-time prosecutor's job and the same as state senator, the mayor's job is full time. Some of the reaction initially was they did not like politics. But now, they enjoy politics. They pay attention to issues and get involved in their own way.

My older daughter went to Girl's Nation from Indiana; my younger daughter was senior class president in high school. They both show some of the same signs of interest.

I grew up with the message politics are good and exciting. It was the way you made the community better. Politics was how you got into government, and government was how you made your community stronger. The commitment was always how do you make the situation better. It was an inclusive view, never my interest group or political party vs. your interest group or political party.

### Barry Goldwater

I went through some stages. Father and grandfather were strong Republicans, and it was reinforced by a lot of my friends. I was a big Barry Goldwater supporter in high school, and that's why I went to the national convention in 1964.

When I went to IU in 1966, it's when anti-war and civil rights movements were becoming bigger on campuses, even at non-radical ones like IU. I tried to go to as many different events as possible. I'd always try to hear as many different speakers and different points of views. It was never my thought I was only going to read Republican or conservative columnists. I remember in high school one of my closest friends was more conservative than I; the close friend was more liberal. It made for good discussion. Some times they'd win, some times you did.

## Divergent voices

I was used to listening to all different sides of an argument. I remember even in high school hearing speakers from the John Birch Society. But I'd also hear Martin Luther King Jr., just about anybody, including Democratic candidates.

It was an important lesson early on: hear what all the sides are saying and get an independent judgment of what was going on. At IU, it was heightened because you'd hear anti-establishment, anti-war speakers, whether it was the Students for a Democratic Society or the Black Panthers.

You had such a splintering, such a profusion of differing points of views in the 1960s. There were so many variations on all sides of the spectrum and I tried to listen to all of them. Listening to those viewpoints, you'd realize what the arguments were going to be. It's one of my skills. I'm good at sensing what the arguments are going to be from differing sides and can figure out the strong and weak points of each. It's something you pick up as a lawyer as well.

*Photo by Helmke family*

**Final day**
The Helmke family—Paul and his wife, Deborah, flanked by daughters Laura, left,

and Kathryn, right—poses at the mayor's desk on the 9th floor of the City-County Building on New Year's Day 2000, Helmke's last day in office. Helmke's daughters traded places from New Year's Day 1988, his first day in the office. (See photo above.)

Even if issues didn't logically make sense, you could sense which ones resonated with an audience. Spellbinding speakers makes you think why are people responding? What is it about the message that's connecting with them? Is it the logic, emotion or self-interest?

It's that part of political discourse that always fascinated me and always has driven my allies, and opponents, crazy. They're never sure where I'm coming from and it's because I'm pretty good at analyzing different approaches.

**Life skills**

The skills you need in politics are the same skills you need in life. Politics are communications, analysis and people skills. For politics, it's important to convey your message. Analytical skills give you a sense of what the issues are and what side you are on. People skills, meanwhile, are just relating to people. It applies to all jobs, especially in the new economy in the 21st century. Those skills are becoming more rare because of the Internet and other forms of communication that have become so impersonal.

There's something in us that just doesn't want to deal with robots or machines. It's what politics is all about. Yet, it's scary in these days of money when you can almost envision a nonhuman, make-believe candidate being able to run a TV campaign and get elected.

## Competing with my father

I don't think I would have done anything differently, although my family would have supported whatever vocation I had chosen. But, in a sense, I was competing with my father. Part of it is being the oldest child, and my parents were very young when I was born. When I learned what my father did in high school or college, I set it as my goal. Not only would I emulate or copy it, I'd try to beat what my father did or would compete with him. Sometimes I did; sometimes I didn't. From my side, it was built into me to do what my father and grandfather had done, and do it better if possible.

Politics has its pitfalls. It was always clear to me; there was a financial cost to it. My father gave up a lot of productive time and years by getting involved in politics. While my father was financially healthy, he was not as financially healthy as his peers who focused on a legal practice or on a business profession. When he was doing politics, it took precedence over the making money side of things.

For my grandfather, it was probably the case as well. Actually, in the Depression, politics was a stabilizing force. To be city attorney during those times meant he had a steady income even if the other guys were paying you with chickens and vegetables.

I grew up comfortably financially, and it's been the same on my own. But my focus has never been on making money. My peers made a lot more money over the years than I. And I knew I was giving it up by running for mayor. It was a lesson I got from my dad and granddad: It's OK. There's more to life than making money.

## Loss of privacy

There was pride from my folks, but also the realization I was giving up some as well. The other cost was the loss of privacy. It's changed over the years and it became more an issue for me than what my parents and grandparents had gone through. In the 1930s and 1940s, when my grand-father was in politics, you didn't have the same loss of privacy as you do today. In my dad's era it was somewhat the same.

Now, you have media, newspapers, talk radio, and a lot more exposure. People are a lot more curious about politicians' private lives, their wealth and their health; those intrusions weren't so common in the old days. It's one of the reasons my dad was concerned about me running for mayor; he saw how politics became a game with a lot more down sides. Win Moses, for example was involved in scandals, and my father saw it as a nasty business.

The one advantage of the mayor's job, however, is being at home. If I was in Congress when my daughters were young, it would have been more of a concern. It's tough to have your family there. Here, even with travel or late hours, I was generally home most of the time. I could still get to the school plays and graduation activities.

By the time I ran for U.S. Senate, the girls were juniors in college and high school so the timing was better. I look at politicians that way; I look at the age of their children and it tells me a lot about what they think of their family or what they're going to put into it. A lot of politicians pass up opportunities because of the age of their children. If they don't pass up the opportunities, there's an extra cost to the family they have to be careful about.

## Used to the spotlight

I was used to the spotlight and had an expectation of what it would be like. I remember college, when Dad was prosecutor around the late 1960s, and having some of my friends over to the house. This is a time my father's a prosecutor and drugs are becoming very prevalent on college campuses. As a result, some of my friends began to wonder whether I was a narc or an informer; not that anybody was actually doing drugs there, but just the suspicion lingered.

I always believed the best thing was to keep my family out of the public eye.

My wife, Debbie, really doesn't like politics. I didn't like using my children as political props either. They'd be in an occasional photo for a political brochure, for example, but even not much of that.

As a result, unless the family really wanted to go to something, I left them out. I wanted the kids to have some privacy; the same with Debbie.

Debbie is a kindergarten teacher at Harrison Hill, and both girls went there. When I first ran, Kathryn might have been in kindergarten, Laura might have been in fourth grade there. For elementary school kids, being the daughter of a teacher is a lot more notorious than being the daughter of a politician. It had a lot more cachet. To these school kids, it was Mrs. Helmke and the "schoolteacher's daughter," not the mayor's daughter. Having that might have shielded them somewhat from being identified as the mayor's kids.

I remember going to the grocery store with Debbie shortly after being elected, and there was one of the kids she had a year before. His parents said to him, "Do you know who that is?" And they're pointing at me. And the kid says, yes, that's Mrs. Helmke's husband.

I wasn't Mayor Helmke; I was Mrs. Helmke's husband.

## Crank calls

We got a lot of crank phone calls. We had set up two phone lines, one in the basement for business; the other, personal. We wanted a listed line so people could reach me.

As a result, some calls were threatening; they gave you an insight into human behavior. It was one aspect of the job as an elected official I didn't enjoy, and neither did my family. We were relieved of that part when I left office. There's a lot of wear and tear with the job.

**Rewarding as well**

Flip side, the job is rewarding. There are parts to it I liked: meeting people, having fun going places.

Often, the family couldn't be part of it because they had their own lives. The parenting aspect was difficult; I always tried to set aside time for the family life and the parental responsibilities, but the time demands of being a mayor made marriage and parenting a problem. You try to get through it but everything you do is magnified.

As a result, it put a strain on my personal life, but it was nobody else's business.

This kind of scrutiny makes it harder for good people to run for office. When you add all these costs—professional, relatively low pay, personal—it makes it tough for anyone to handle. Under that kind of microscope, it makes things tricky.

Your ego also tells you that you like walking the tightrope and living on the edge. There's an excitement when you don't know quite where events are leading.

I miss the job but it was time to move on. Being mayor's one of the greatest jobs in the world. It's a good feeling despite the pressures on the family. I'm a better person for it and hopefully better for my family.

**'Hit the road, Jack'**

The job also came with a lot of funny stories.

There was the time Ray Charles came to town. Some local promoter brought Charles to sing at the Franke Park outdoor theater. I always liked Ray Charles so I was excited about this. Barb Nussa, who was doing my scheduling then, was a good scheduler and she felt this was an exciting event. We did a key to the city for it; we didn't do many of these and less afterward.

The promoter, however, didn't have the money put together for the show. And Ray Charles is there and he's backstage and I'm backstage. He's in one of these back rooms and he's basically saying that unless he gets another several grand, he wasn't going to sing. The guy didn't have the money, and he's running around scrambling trying to find some more bucks. There's a decent crowd of several thousand people, and they're getting unhappy as Ray Charles is getting unhappy. I'm backstage saying to myself, "This is getting embarrassing."

It's the tricky part of being mayor; you're connected with a lot that you have no control over.

I'm there but I didn't put this together. I didn't ask this guy about the finances or anything; this is a private venture.

So it gets to the point where Charles has waited about 45 minutes, the crowd's getting unruly and the promoter's trying to spin all sorts of things. Finally, Ray decides he's leaving.

"Can't you come out and say, 'Hi', maybe sing one song," I'm thinking. But I understand from his perspective: I don't get paid, I don't sing.

He walked out, but at least I had a chance to meet him. He was gracious; I wasn't the problem. I think I gave the key to him anyway; what else was I going to do with it?

It was too bad how the situation turned out.

To me it was a lesson. It's real easy to get caught up in other people's problems as mayor; I wasn't going to bail the guy out with money from the city. I might have paid for my ticket if it would have made a difference. But this guy messed over the audience, the city, Ray Charles and me.

I told Barb Nussa afterward we're going to watch these things a lot more closely. There are a lot of folks who have ideas, whether it's entertainment or economic development, that don't work out like they're supposed to.

**Everyone wants the mayor**

It's real hard to have a rule of thumb about where you go and where you don't. It all depends on a good scheduler who's hearing these schemes first-hand. There are so many requests, you get swamped. I tried to have two nights a week clear, and would do things during those nights but only if I signed off on them ahead of time.

It was the same with weekends.

However, in an election year, you say yes to just about everything because you want to be visible. And then you're really swamped.

I'd get to the stage where I knew I had attended similar events more so than the organizers of these events. They'd say, "The mayor's never been to our event." I'd respond "I was there four years ago, seven years ago. You don't remember when I was there."

I always had to get the family schedule done first before doing the mayoral schedule so the two would fit as best as possible. Scheduling was one of the toughest parts of the job; folks expected you to be there.

We put together a question sheet when these requests came up for people to answer. What's this all about? What's the mayor's role? How many people are expected? How long will it last? Can I get in and out, or am I expected to stay the entire time? Those were always tough decisions.

The estimates were amazing. They'd say 400 people; you'd get there, and there were 40. But people were trying to get you there, thus the inflated estimates. You had to realize as mayor, by attending, you were giving an event validity and exposure, often from the media. A lot of TV stations decided where to go based on a weekly schedule of events I had made available.

## A real fun job

The job also allowed me to pick things that were fun. "This sounds like fun, and I'm being invited because I am mayor."

I saw the job as a once-in-a-lifetime opportunity and I wanted to take advantage of it. I believed I had been active in the community and knew things before I became mayor. But there were things going on I didn't realize were out there.

To wear a kilt at Scottish Highland Days, for example, and to march in the Three Rivers Parade, and to hang from the monkey nets at the zoo, throw out a ball at a Wizards games, drop the puck at a Komets game, it's so exciting to do these things.

I threw out the ball twice at Chicago's Wrigley Field. It was the most nervous I had ever been, and this includes being on national TV, introducing the president and being a contestant on "Jeopardy!"

The first time I threw out the ball at the stadium, there were 30,000 people, although not more than 20 were probably looking at me because I was no big deal. So I'm on the mound throwing out this pitch, and it's my windup, and the catcher's Damon Berryhill, who didn't last long before moving onto the Braves, and he's coming out of a crouch to catch it. My pitch is high but it's over the plate. And I remember winding up and I remember him catching it. I don't remember throwing the ball; I had blanked out. It was the most nervous I had ever been.

There, I wanted to do it right. Wrigley Field was the hallowed confines; that was fun.

I remember telling local attorney John Walda I'd be throwing out a pitch at Wrigley Field. Walda said if he had known the mayor could do that, he'd have run for office.

**Tough being gone**

I do miss the people. While it's nice to look at my schedule and see how I'm home evenings, weekends, and didn't have to go to Cinco de Mayo or Arbor Day or the North vs. South Civil War re-enactment. But I liked doing those things.

There's always a flip side; there are tremendous demands on your time but you also like doing it. It would still be nice to go to things, although I still do some as ex-mayor.

It's tough being gone. It was more exciting than what I'm doing now as an attorney at Barnes & Thornburg. It would be more exciting than almost any job you could have. You were always on your toes; you never knew what was going to happen. The challenge was fun. Walking the tightrope, living on the edge, that was exciting. I've been telling people it was like doing a treadmill going 100 mph.

I was handling it and doing a good job, and could have kept on doing it. But I knew sooner or later, I would burn out. That's why I decided not to run. Sooner or later, I'd get bored with it—at least with some facets—and then I wouldn't be doing a very good job for the city and its citizens. It's when you start making mistakes.

**Going out on top**

It's like watching a star athlete; I wanted to come out on top. I could have been a good productive mayor, but after a while, you realize you're doing something over and over again. After a while, you don't want to be the old fogey saying, "This is the way we used to do things" or "We thought about this idea before and rejected it for these reasons."

It would be a sign I was losing my edge and sharpness. And it's not fair to the city or to me. I figured there'd be challenges for me in the private sector, and I'm still looking for them.

**Run again?**

I've had people ask me if I would ever run again for mayor. I doubt it.

Look at the history of Fort Wayne mayors. Few served as long as I did. Both of the mayors who served at least 12 years like I—Harry Baals in the 1930s, 40s and 50s, and Charles Zollinger, in the latter part of the 19th century—stepped down and then ran again. And both died in office after they came back. I told people, "Remind me, that if I think about running for mayor again, what happened to Zollinger and Baals when they came back."

Now, I'm making more money. I'm home a lot more. I'm more in control of my schedule, whereas in the past, your schedule controlled you. I don't worry as much about media coverage as I did when mayor, when I wanted to see what they were saying about me. I still pay attention, but now more about events related to my era. If it's what the new guys are doing, I'm not going to comment unless it relates to my legacy.

**A proud man**

I'm really proud of my legacy and how we left the city. You can't live in the past, but I worked with good people that I try to keep in touch with. When something comes up that tries to tarnish the legacy and the work done by other people, I might comment on it.

With the passage of time, I'll become more distant from affairs. People will stop pointing fingers at me. I've always liked people to pay attention to me when I speak up, because generally I believe my opinions are worth listening to. When you're mayor, people do that.

I hope they still stay pay attention to me statewide or locally after being out of office. Hopefully, it's the ideas that count, not just the office.

## Cast of characters:

**Walter P. Helmke**—Paul Helmke's father and currently a local attorney, he was the Republican Party's unsuccessful candidate for Congress in 1974

**Walter E. Helmke**—Paul Helmke's grandfather, he was elected Allen County prosector in 1928

**Barry Goldwater**—Long-time conservative Arizona senator, he ran unsuccessfully for President against Lyndon Johnson in 1964

# ABOUT THE AUTHOR

Andrew Jarosh is a journalist at the Fort Wayne (Ind.) News-Sentinel, where he covered the Paul Helmke administration. A graduate of the University of Wisconsin system with a Master's degree in communications, he also has done consulting overseas and hopes to write a book about Nazi victims and collaborators in Eastern Europe during World War II.

0-595-21600-5